MISSION IN THE THIRD MILLENNIUM

MISSION
in the
Third Millennium

Robert J. Schreiter
Editor

ORBIS BOOKS

Maryknoll, New York 10545

Second Printing, August 2002

Founded in 1970, Orbis Books endeavors to publish works that enlighten the mind, nourish the spirit, and challenge the conscience. The publishing arm of the Maryknoll Fathers and Brothers, Orbis seeks to explore the global dimensions of the Christian faith and mission, to invite dialogue with diverse cultures and religious traditions, and to serve the cause of reconciliation and peace. The books published reflect the views of their authors and do not represent the official position of the Society.

To learn more about Maryknoll and Orbis Books, please visit our website at www.maryknoll.com.

Library of Congress Cataloging-in-Publication Data

Mission in the third millennium / edited by Robert J. Schreiter.
    p. cm.
    Papers presented at a meeting.
    Includes bibliographical references and index.
    ISBN 1-57075-368-7
    1. Missions. I. Schreiter, Robert J.

BV2061 .M565 2001
266'.2'09051—dc21

                        2001034023

Contents

107079

Preface

THE TURN OF THE MILLENNIUM IN THE CHRISTIAN CALENDAR was not simply an opportunity to rethink the direction of Christian mission. Important changes in the world through the 1990s made such a rethinking genuinely necessary. The realignment of the world's political order, the advent of globalization, the shifting of sources of missionary personnel all pointed toward significant changes that needed to be taken into consideration. While secularization continued to advance in many of the world's societies, the world was at the same time more religious than had been the case a few decades ago. Religion found itself bound up with ethnicity and with violence in many places. Pentecostalism and a variety of fundamentalisms had also changed the face of religion in many places. All in all, so much had changed in the context of mission that its direction needed to be refocused.

For that reason, SEDOS convened a congress in Rome, April 3-8, 2000, on the future of mission. SEDOS (*Servizio de Documentazione e Studi,* Center for Documentation and Study) is an organization sponsored by some one hundred missionary congregations of men and women in the Roman Catholic Church. Founded in 1966 in the wake of the Second Vatican Council, SEDOS has as its purpose to be a documentation and study resource to the congregations that sponsor it, and indeed to the wider church. A mission seminar is sponsored annually, as well as lectures and study groups throughout the year. It publishes a monthly bulletin which reprints some of the best recent literature on mission. It also houses a small library with an especially good periodical collection on mission-related topics.

Along with these regular services, SEDOS has undertaken from time to time to sponsor larger gatherings to examine the direction of mission. In 1969, at a time when the "why" of mission was under considerable debate, it sponsored a meeting of theologians and missionaries to explore the motives for mission and the consequences that needed to be drawn for the conduct of mission. In 1981, SEDOS sponsored a ten-day research seminar on the future of mission, involving over one hundred missionaries and theologians. The agenda for future planning and research that came out of that seminar effectively defined the future direction of mission for the next two decades. Under the headings of proclamation, dialogue, inculturation, and liberation of the poor, the agenda sought to define the "how" of mission as it would be carried out in the final years of the twentieth century.

In the mission congress for 2000, six speakers were invited to look at current issues in mission from the perspectives of the continents of Asia, Africa, Europe, Latin America, and North America. After each presentation, one of the other speakers responded with perspectives on the same issues from his or her point of view. This was all taken into some sixteen small groups, working in five different languages, to allow participants to pursue the issues further. All in all, over two hundred people participated in each day's proceedings.

The presentations and the responses are presented in this volume. There is, in addition, a final essay, which draws together some of the principal themes that emerged in the congress. That essay also includes the results of the small group discussions. What emerges is a picture of a stimulating six days of discussion and dialogue.

Many hands go into the planning and directing of a congress held on this scale and into the preparation of the proceedings. Thanks must go first of all to Walter von Holzen, S.V.D., executive director of SEDOS. He conceived the idea and the format of the congress and made contact with the speakers. He oversaw the many details of the congress itself, as well as its smooth execution. The Executive Committee of SEDOS not only gave approval for the congress, but gave it constant support through the planning and the process of the meeting itself. Gratitude must be expressed also to SEDOS for technical support. Carolyn Perz of the Bernardin Center at Catholic Theological Union in Chicago gave invaluable help in the preparation of the manuscript for publication. And perhaps most of all, thanks go to the participants in the congress for making it such a stimulating and thought-provoking event.

ROBERT J. SCHREITER, C.PP.S.
Chicago
February 14, 2001

Contributors

Michael Amaladoss, S.J., is professor of theology at Vidyajyoti College of Theology in Delhi, India. He served for twelve years as assistant to the superior general of the Jesuits, and is a past president of the International Association of Mission Studies. He has also served as a consultant to the Pontifical Council for Interreligious Dialogue.

María Carmelita de Freitas, F.I., is professor of theology at the Center for Higher Studies of the Jesuits in Belo Horizonte, Brazil. She has long been involved in work with the religious congregations of Brazil at the national level. Currently she is a member of the team of theologians for the Conference of Religious of Brazil, and holds a similar position with CLAR, the Latin American Association of Religious.

Sung-Hae Kim, S.C., is professor in the department of religious studies at Sogang University, in South Korea, where she specializes in Chinese religion. She is also director of the Tasan Research Center in Kangjin, and currently serves as Provincial in Korea of the Sisters of Charity of Seton Hill.

Peter Hünermann is professor emeritus of dogmatic theology at the University of Tübingen in Germany. He is the founding president (and now honorary president) of the European Society of Catholic Theology. He is a priest of the diocese of Aachen.

Mercy Amba Oduyoye is director of the Institute of African Women in Religion and Culture at Trinity Theological College in Legon, Ghana. For many years she taught in the department of religious studies at the University of Ibadan in Nigeria. She is currently president of the Ecumenical Association of Third World Theologians, and served as deputy general secretary of the World Council of Churches.

Robert J. Schreiter, C.PP.S., is professor of theology at Catholic Theological Union in Chicago, Illinois, U.S.A. He is past president of the American Society of Missiology and of the Catholic Theological Society of America. He is general editor of the Faith and Cultures Series of Orbis Books. He is a member of the Missionaries of the Precious Blood and serves on its general council.

1

An East Asian Understanding of Mission and the Future of the Christian Presence

Sung-Hae Kim, S.C.

I WOULD LIKE TO BEGIN WITH MY PERSONAL EXPERIENCE. My congregation, the Sisters of Charity of Seton Hill, whose motherhouse is located in Greensburg, Pennsylvania, sent ten long-term missionaries to Korea from 1960 to 1984 when the Korean mission/region was established as a province. Among the ten, six of the sisters chose to go back to the United States at different stages, while four sisters continued to stay with us, providing their quiet presence of faithful lives or offering the role of bridge builders. What made me stop and think was the interesting phenomenon that it was generally the former group of the sisters who had the dream of being missionaries from their youth, but at the same time felt threatened by the growing number of native sisters. I still remember the frank comment of one sister just before she left Korea: "Koreans will make the decisions on the future of the Korean mission, so I better go back." On the other hand, one of the sisters from the latter group who stayed with us, does not like the title "missionary"; rather she insists that she is a Christian who wants to share in the life of other people and their culture wherever divine providence guides her. This latter understanding seems to me nearer to the original concept of mission spoken and lived by Jesus and which we can meet with the East Asian insights such as the Confucian notion of the Mandate of Heaven and the Taoist sage, who equalizes everything under heaven.

When the Sisters came to Korea in 1960 to start a girls' high school in a little country town named Kangjin, what people needed were scientific skills, pianos, folk dances, and a knowledge of English. Now all these things are provided by the government and private academies in the town. After forty years what the people in Kangjin want from the Christian and religious presence has changed. As this small example shows, we have to probe for the future of the Christian presence in the developed societies with highly sophisticated cultural traditions such as Korea, Japan, China, and the other East Asian countries. The direction in which our religious congregation is heading seems to be a token of how the missionary church should go in the twenty-first century. Now we are composed of about 500 members, 300 Americans and 200 Koreans. In an extraordinary chapter that was held in July 1999, simultaneously in the two countries, we decided to establish two equal, parallel provinces with the overarching general government composed of an equitable number of officers. Moreover, the Korean community began to interpret our charism, which originated from St. Elizabeth Seton and St. Vincent de Paul, with the cultural language of East Asia, that is, with Confucian, Taoist, and Buddhist insights. I believe the mutual acceptance of viewing our charism from different cultural perspectives is the deepest exchange a religious community can experience and so it offers an excellent witness to the future mode of Christian mission. Now I will venture to look at the concept of mission from the perspectives of two native traditions of East Asia, Confucianism and Taoism.

The Confucian Notion of the Mandate of Heaven and the Personal Concept of Mission

The religious foundation of Confucian teaching is the unconditional faith in heaven, as the ultimate source of all beings and of moral principles, which governs both the human and cosmic world. The earliest written material which expresses this faith and which has been repeatedly quoted by the numerous Confucians throughout the centuries is a famous phrase from the *Book of Poetry* edited around 600 B.C.E.: "Heaven gave birth to the multitude of people, and so whenever there is a being, there is a principle of life which governs it. People hold rightness in their heart and love beautiful virtue" (Ode 260).[1] Heaven is regarded here as the source of human life which has bestowed moral nature as the core of human constitutions. Mencius (372-289 B.C.E.) quoted this phrase in order to support his theory of the goodness of human nature and added the mission of the first awakened people: "Heaven, in producing the people, has given to those who first attain understanding the duty of awakening those who are slow to understand" (5A7). The Doctrine of the Mean developed it into the typical Confucian definition of nature: "What Heaven commanded is called nature" (1,1).

Chong Yagyong (1762-1836), who is better known by his pen name, Tasan, Tea Mountain, wrote the most dynamic commentary on the above opening phrase of the Doctrine of the Mean: "What heaven commanded is nature, and so we can talk about it in terms of tendencies. When a human being is conceived, heaven bestows on it the spiritual brightness which is without form. Therefore, a human being naturally likes the good and abhors evil" (*The Complete Works of Tasan,* II-3, 2b).[2]

In Confucianism this heaven-endowed moral nature rooted in every human heart is the foundation of human responsibility. In other words, every human person is believed to have the ability to cultivate his/her personality and become a virtuous person as the man/woman of benevolence.

While this first connotation of the Mandate of Heaven is a universal call inasmuch as it is a moral responsibility based on human nature, the second usage of the Mandate of Heaven is a command given to particular persons in each unique situation.

---

[1] I consulted for this translation *The Book of Odes,* trans. Bernard Karlgren (Stockholm: Museum of Far East Antiquities, 1974), 228.

[2] The English translation is mine. For the thought of Tasan, see my article "Chong Yagyong (Tasan): Creative Bridge Between the East and the West," in *Confucian Philosophy in Korea,* ed. Haei Chang Choung (Academy of Korean Studies, 1996), 213-91. I think his commentary is more dynamic and closer to the text than the Neo-Confucian understanding of nature as the unchangeable principle.

The aforementioned Tasan, the synthesizer of the Korean Confucian school of practical learning, pointed out this second connotation very clearly, quoting the second phrase of the first stanza of Ode 260: "Heaven looks after our country (Chou) and spreads out the light in the world. It gave birth to a wise minister (Chung Shanfu) to protect our Son of Heaven." Tasan distinguishes between the birth of the multitude of people and the birth of a wise minister, for the first birth indicated the universal caring of all beings, while the second birth carries the meaning of the providential care.[3] What interests me here is the fact that this providential sense of the Mandate of Heaven is quite similar to the Christian concept of charism as a divine gift given to particular persons in order to build up the community as a whole. The charism of a religious as well as the charism given to a religious community can be viewed in this latter sense of the Mandate of Heaven.

These two dimensions of the Confucian notion of the Mandate of Heaven can be applied to the understanding of Christian mission. The primary and universal mission of every Christian is to recover and perfect the image of God that is given as the core nature and the foundation of human dignity. We bear witness to God insofar as we achieve the benevolent image of God in us. This kind of witness transcends the various states, vocations, and roles that each one of us is called to serve in the church. In the history of the Catholic Church the canonized saints who come from various walks of life best symbolize this primary and universal witness, that is, mission. The second and particular mission is directly related to charism, the concept of gift or grace from God given specifically for a particular purpose. If we approach the concept of grace in this sense, in connection with the primary Mandate of Heaven for the people as a whole, even the Confucians will be able to comprehend why it is not a selfish desire or private interest to pray for the grace of God. The critics of the

---

[3] Tasan's *Lectures on the Book of Poetry*, III, 34a. The following books may be useful: Tu Weiming, *Centrality and Commonality* (Honolulu: University Press of Hawaii, 1976), and various articles and other books by the same author; Sung-Hae Kim, *Primitive Confucianism: Hermeneutical Approach to the Analects, Mencius, and Hsu ntzu* (in Korean) (Mimumsa, 1990), 61.

early Jesuits working in China found it very hard to reconcile the universal love of God and the concept of grace given to a few.

In other words, placing two concepts—the Confucian concept of the Mandate of Heaven as the universal moral nature, and the life command to particular people—along with the Christian concept of universal *imago Dei* and particular charism, deepens mutual understanding. The comparison clarifies different connotations each tradition carries with it. In both cases the first connotation is universal and applied to humanity as a whole and even extends to the cosmos. The second connotation is the heavenly command[4] or the graced calling of the merciful God to help people to achieve the primary mandate. The particular commands, therefore, are closely connected with the universal mandate and are really a tool to achieve the primary mission to be fully human and to form a benevolent society and cosmos.

The Taoist Image of Self-Transformation and the Social Concept of Mission

The central teaching of Lao Tzu, the founder of the Taoist school in the sixth century B.C.E., is that the workings of the Tao (literally, the Way, which is the ultimate reality and the principle of the universe) is neither oppressive nor competitive, but rather natural and merciful. Because the Tao runs the universe naturally with non-action (*wu-wei*), it encourages all beings to be self-transformative, self-enriching, and self-supportive. The sage who follows the Tao, therefore, nurtures and perfects everything without possessing them as his own. The book of Lao Tzu, which is called *Tao Te Ching* (The Classic of the Way and Its Power), shows us the social mission of the sage as follows:

---

[4] In the Confucian tradition, the heavenly command is not as much talked about as in the Christian tradition. But one of the best examples can be found in Mencius 6B15: "That is why Heaven, when it is about to place a great burden on man, always first tests his resolution, exhausts his frame and makes him suffer starvation and hardship, frustrates his efforts so as to shake him from his mental lassitude, toughen his nature and make good his deficiencies. As a rule, a man can mend his ways only after he has made mistakes. It is only when a man is frustrated in mind and in his deliberations that he is able to innovate" (Penguin, 181).

Is not the way of heaven like the stretching of a bow? The high it presses down, the low it lifts up; the excessive it takes from, the deficient it gives to. It is the way of heaven to take from what has in excess in order to make good what is deficient. The way of man is otherwise. It takes from those who are in want in order to offer this to those who already have more than enough. Who is there that can take what he/she himself/herself has in excess and offer this to the empire? Only he/she who has the way. (chapter 77)[5]

The sage aims for the equitable society where everyone has what he/she needs. Lao Tzu knew, however, that the level of people's need is limitless, and so it is of paramount importance for the sage to teach them to appreciate simplicity of life-style and stillness of mind by taking the value of the Tao. In chapter 4 Lao Tzu recommends that the leaders of society should learn to be like one of the people: "Blunt your sharpness, untangle the knots, soften your glare, and become one with the dusty world." By lowering oneself and becoming one of the people, the sage is able to gradually purify the dirty waters of the world. In chapter 15, Lao Tzu portrays this purification process: "Who can be muddy and yet, settling, slowly become limpid? Who can be at rest and yet, stirring, slowly come to life?"

This Taoist image of the sage who becomes one with the world so that he/she may gradually purify the corruptions of the world and stir up the life of the Tao on this earth is much like the mission of Jesus and his followers. This kind of mission has a social character, and only those who are firmly grounded in the gospel values are capable of carrying it out. That might be the reason why the concluding remark of *Tao Te Ching* chapter 15 is, "He/she who holds fast to this way desires not to be full." Emptiness, or humility, keeps both the Taoist sage and the Christian faithful to the original insight. Lao Tzu loves to use natural examples to teach a true value of the social usefulness of emptying oneself and one's selfish desires. Water, which flows down and loves to stay in the lower place; the empty vessel, which can hold various foods; the empty space of the building, which gives us room to dwell;

---

[5] *Tao Te Ching*, trans. D. C. Lau (Chinese University Press), 111.

and the empty area of musical instruments, which makes it possible for air to go through—all these natural signs of the Tao point us toward getting rid of our selfish concerns and opening our vision for the bigger picture.

The mission of the Taoist sage is not aggressive, but only helps a spontaneous flowering to happen. The *Tao Te Ching* chapter 57 describes the sage thus:

> I take no action and the people are transformed of themselves;
> I prefer stillness and the people are rectified of themselves;
> I am not meddlesome and the people prosper of themselves;
> I am free from desire and the people of themselves become simple like the uncarved block.

The uncarved block is one of the major symbols of the Tao, signifying its primary simplicity and original state of life energy and beauty. It sounds a little idealistic, but isn't it the main principle of Christian social teaching as well? The goal of any social welfare program is to help the needy be self-supportive and self-governing, so the people will gain a true respect for themselves and their culture. In chapter 61 Lao Tzu illustrates a desired relationship between the large state and the small state: "The large should take the lower position." Just as the ocean stands lower than the rivers, the large and powerful religio-cultural unit should not be aggressive in its missionary activities. In order to fulfill the social mission compassionately, therefore, one has to be really mature and virtuous, so that all sides can live together comfortably in a mutually respectful atmosphere of each other, both individually and communally.

The Taoist understanding of social mission teaches us to deepen our concept of mission. How aggressive have we Christians been toward other religious traditions in East Asia? More than aggressive—sometimes we were oppressive and even destructive of others in the name of Christian mission. Only recently have we been trying to reconcile the concept of mission with that of dialogue. Respectful coexistence with nature as well as with other human communities is something we have to learn from the Taoist spirit of nonaction. If we truly trust the providence of God in cosmic and human history, we Christians have to be a little more patient and humbler before the mystery of cosmos and human complexities. The social mission of the Christian Church will be accomplished only when we cooperate with other religions to make our world more equitable, freer from aggressive desires of material comforts, and more respectful of various cultural inheritors of this earth.

A Historical Reflection on Missionary Activities in East Asia

I have been teaching for the last twenty years at Sogang University in Seoul on the encounter between East Asian religious traditions and Christianity. Last year, I finally published my work in book form.[6] Focusing on the concept of mission, I would like here to reflect on a few major encounters in East Asia during 450 years: the first arrival of Francesco Xavier in Japan in 1549, the dedication of the world map to the Chinese emperor by Matteo Ricci in 1603, and the baptism of the first Korean seeker of faith, Yi Sunghun, at a Beijing Catholic church in 1784.

Japan

The Jesuits in Japan, who first explored the missionary possibilities for Christian gospel values in the heavily intertwined Buddhist-Shinto culture of the sixteenth century, showed an ambivalent attitude toward Japanese tradition. In one way the Jesuits took Japanese Zen masters as their role models by assuming similar robes, social standing, and cultural refinement such as training in the tea ceremony. Accepting the Zen masters as equivalent spiritual teachers, the Jesuits, including Xavier and Cosme de Torres, carried on interreligious dialogue, even though in crucial matters such as interdependent coorigination and immortal-

---

[6] My reflections here are based on my book *Encounter between East Asian Religious Traditions and Christianity* (in Korean) (Spiritual Life Press, 1999). I regret that I could not include Vietnam in my research owing to the lack of available material.

ity of the soul, both sides had difficulty in understanding each other. On the other hand, even the Jesuits, in spite of all their humanistic training, looked negatively on Japanese native tradition, Shinto, and its multivalent concept of *kami* (superior powers or deities). One of the most agonizing things for the early Jesuits in Japan was their awareness that their first chosen name of God, Dainichi, the honorific title of the sun goddess Amaterasu, was a created deity during the mythic time and regarded by the Japanese Buddhists only as the Japanese manifestation of Vairocana Buddha.[7] As soon as they realized their mistake, they chose to use the Latin form of God, *Deus*, in its transliteration. Since Japanese native culture does not have the clear notion of one supreme deity or High God, their difficulty is understandable. However, offering the most crucial name of God in a transliterated foreign term was never successful, and it stayed for centuries as the symbol of the foreignness of Christianity in Japan, an impression from which Japanese Christianity is not completely free even today.

Persecution of Christians and the abrupt rupture of Christian missionary activity in seventeenth-century Japan were due more to political factors than to a religious failure. But when Christianity was reintroduced in 1859 in a Protestant form, and also partly revived in its Catholic form, it was Japanese Protestant churches that first took the native name *kami* for the Christian name of God. Japanese Catholics followed this choice much later. A contemporary Catholic novelist, Endo Shusaku, attempted a soul-searching effort to harmonize the Christian concept of God with the native notion of *kami* through his historical novel *Silence* and his *Life of Jesus*.[8] For him the concept of a powerful God who conquers and wins all the time, just like the imperial powers of the West, does not appeal to the hearts of the Japanese. He tried to find a tender and motherly side of God in the life of the historical Jesus, who becomes weak and suffers with the suffering people. According to him, only in this suffering and merciful face of God will the Japanese find some resonance with

---

[7] For a concise explanation of Vairocana Buddha, see "Vairocana," in *The Perennial Dictionary of World Religions*, ed. Keith Crim (New York: Harper & Row, 1989).

[8] Both books are translated into Korean and English as well.

their own meaning of *kami*. In other words, he is saying that unless Japanese Christianity inculturates itself into Japanese soil and spirituality, there is no hope for the Christian mission in Japan. I do not know whether he is right or wrong, but the fact that presently the total Christian population including both Catholics and Protestants does not exceed more than one percent indicates that Christian witness value is meager in a society that is very westernized and modernized in other aspects.

China

It is well known that when Michele Ruggieri wrote the first catechism in Chinese in 1583, he took Buddhism as the bridge, but Matteo Ricci, who also participated in the first catechism, soon realized that it was Confucianism which held the position of orthodoxy in China. Consequently, when he composed the famous *True Meaning of God* in 1596, Ricci chose Confucianism as his dialogue partner and took Confucian notions of High God and human perfection as the starting points for the Christian teaching. His famous statement that "God whom we teach is the same Lord of Heaven whom the Confucian Classics teach" summarizes his attitude toward Chinese culture. Ricci saw that among the three religions of China, while the core of Buddhism is emptiness and that of Taoism is nothingness, only Confucianism teaches reality and sincere living in this world. Therefore Ricci concluded that Confucian teaching is nearer to truth and that Christianity which he brought to China is able to supplement and perfect it.

Ricci's success was due to his sympathetic approach to the Confucian classics and his humanistic exchange of the cultural heritage—as we know by the fact that his first treatise, *On Friendship,* was warmly accepted by the contemporary Chinese literati as a whole. Actually, after reading it, they gave him the honorific title, a "Western Confucian scholar." His success was partial, however, for his understanding of Buddhism and Taoism was poor, and his attitude toward popular culture was quite negative. This negative look at the Chinese cultural symbols was enlarged and strengthened by the rites controversy among the Jesuits themselves, then between the Jesuits and the Franciscans/Dominicans, and finally between the papacy and the Chinese emperor in the early years of the eighteenth century. The three major issues in this rites controversy were the annual sacrifice to heaven as a thanksgiving for life, the seasonal rites to ancestors, and the Confucian ceremony in honor of the sage Confucius.

Ricci allowed these rites to the new Chinese Christians, for he judged them to be cultural symbols of filial piety and devotion to the cultural hero that could be christianized. But later, stricter interpreters took them to be idol worship that should be rejected in order to be a Christian. During this controversy the Chinese emperor Kangxi, who once was quite favorable toward the Jesuit contribution, officially forbade Christianity in 1721, and the papacy decreed excommunication on those who performed the Chinese rites in 1742.[9] I am looking back to this well-known incident because the rites controversy is not yet over, even though the papal excommunication and the official edict to forbid Christian missionary activity have been lifted. The spirit of the rites controversy stays with us as long as Christian disrespect and lack of appreciation for the Chinese cultural identity continues, and correspondingly the Chinese feeling of being invaded by outside powers whether political, economic, cultural, or spiritual.

As far as I can see, it is not that important whether the missionary agents are Asian, American, African, or European. The Chinese people and the Chinese church want to build up their own community with their own hands, preserving their cultural pride. Outside help is welcomed as long as this basic condition is met. It is crucial for us to remember that one word that has been most important in the spiritual history of China is "culture." From the earliest written record of their history, the Chinese called their country the "middle kingdom," signifying that they are the center of the civilized world. Generally this was true until the sixteenth century, even though now we know that cultural influences were mutual between the central circle of China and the small circles of neighboring countries. The identity of being Chinese is to inherit the cultural heritage of China, which was concretized in the Chinese rites. The details of the rites have been changed greatly during the last hundred years, but the spirit and

---

[9] A good source book is George Minamiki, *The Chinese Rites Controversy: From Its Beginning to Modern Times* (Chicago: Loyola University Press, 1985).

the pride of the Chinese cultural identity continue in the hearts of the people.

After the open-door policy was adopted by the Chinese government, five religions—Buddhism, Taoism, Islam, Catholicism, and Protestantism—were officially recognized and supposedly included approximately 10 percent of the total population.[10] It is interesting that the number of Chinese Buddhists and Taoists is not included within the 10 percent and that Confucianism is not regarded as one of five official religions. Confucianism is now looked upon by the present government leaders as the backbone of cultural heritage, and the works of the contemporary Neo-Confucian scholars such as Mou Tsungsan are widely circulated and studied through the government research fund. Tu Weiming, Harvard professor of Chinese philosophy, has endeavored to make Neo-Confucianism understandable to Western intellectuals and has been actively involved in interreligious dialogue with Christian theologians. In a nut shell, what Tu Weiming points out is that the Confucian emphasis on immanent transcendence in a human heart as the principle of heaven, and the Christian concentration of transcendental transcendence as the personal God, can be mutually beneficial to enlarge our human understanding of the ultimate. The former safeguards room for moral autonomy and focuses our attention on the maturity of the human personality, while the latter provides dynamic energy for social justice by valuing the relational quality between the ultimate and the human. If we learn to appreciate each other's insights on the ultimate truth as well as in the process of cultivation of humanity, we will truly begin a new age of dialogue. Are we Christians and our concept of mission ready for this new age?

Korea

Christianity was introduced to Korea not by missionaries but by Chinese books written by Matteo Ricci and other Jesuits. Christian teaching as well as Western scientific knowledge was

---

[10] *Studies on World Religions* (Beijing; in Chinese) no. 3 (1989): 138. Also see Luo Zhufeng, *Religion under Socialism in China*, trans. Donald Macinnis and Zeng Xian (M.E. Sharpe, 1991).

called by the Koreans at that time a "Western learning," for they were introduced together by the Jesuits, who were both missionaries and scientists. The world map drawn by Ricci was brought in very early by a diplomatic emissary from the Chinese court to the Korean court, and it opened the eyes of Korean intellectuals. The young Confucian scholars who longed for practical learning to reform the ailing society sent their representatives to the missionaries in Beijing to find out more about Catholicism. The fact that Koreans came first to seek the gospel continues to color the active character of Christian mission in Korea and might be the fundamental reason why Christianity has flourished most in Korea among Asian countries other than the Philippines, where Christianity was imposed as a part of colonial policy. Especially when the first Protestant missionaries, H. G. Underwood and H. G. Appenzeller, arrived in Korea in 1885, Korea was just starting to be modernized, and their contribution to modern medical hospitals and modern education for both boys and girls was deeply appreciated by the society as a whole. Christian missionaries' initial assistance for the independence of the nation is a part of the favorable memory for the Korean public even today.

Another positive impact the Christian community has made in recent history is the outspoken defense of human rights against dictatorial governments during the 1970s and the 1980s. It was a hard and precarious struggle for some Korean bishops, priests, religious, and Protestant ministers, but this voice of conscience at a time when no one dared to speak out impressed on the hearts of people that Christians have a genuine concern for justice and the courage to defend it. After the Second Vatican Council, Catholics opened the doors of their hearts toward other religious believers, and this openness is greatly appreciated. In spite of all these positive features of Korean Christianity, a historian of religion recently commented in an academic symposium that, although Christianity might be at the top of the religious map in Korea in both its political and economic power, it still remains culturally marginal. At the center of Korean culture are Buddhism and Confucianism along with folk beliefs mixed with Shamanism and Taoism at the bottom. How can we Christians move to the center of our culture? One thing, of course, is time, but time alone will not lead us to the center of Korean spirituality. This is the common task for the Christians to achieve in East Asia as our societies progress more rapidly and immediate human needs are fulfilled without help from the churches.

The Future of the Christian Presence in East Asia

The dream that the Holy Spirit of God has inspired in the hearts of East Asians for twenty-five hundred years through the voices of the Confucian and Taoist spiritual masters was a continual search for human perfection both individual and communal. The core insight of Confucius was that the destiny of every human person is to cultivate one's moral power, which is endowed by Heaven, so that he/she may provide peace around him/her. The atmosphere of peace and harmony exists wherever the benevolent person resides. The benevolent society where people can joyfully live their full life is the Confucian utopia. Chu Hsi, the synthesizer of Neo-Confucianism in the twelfth century, rephrased this social utopia as "the benevolent and long life milieu," and proposed it as the goal that every Confucian official should work for. Even though Confucianism has been severely criticized for its conservative character, we have to distinguish between its ideal and its adaptation or misuse by self-seeking politicians of various generations. The Confucian dream may not be initiated *by* the people, but it is clearly *for* the people, aiming at building an equitable and benevolent society. As Christians, we have to recognize this and work together to realize this universal dream.

What we can offer is the religious energy and assurance of grace. Matteo Ricci sensed it and insisted that Christianity would replace Buddhism and supplement what is lacking in Confucianism. In order to do this, however, he desired to go back to primitive Confucianism, where the personal concept of the Lord on High is clearly preserved in the Confucian classics. He rejected not only Buddhism and Taoism but also the reinterpretation of Neo-Confucianism. It is not fair for us, however, to deny the historical development of Confucian thought. As Julia Ching pointed out, we have to appreciate the Neo-Confucian emphasis on the immanent understanding of the ultimate.[11] This appreciation will also lead Christians to revive the image of the immanent presence of God in the mystical traditions of the Catholic Church such as the thought of St. Teresa of Avila as well as in the central doctrine of divinization of the Eastern Churches. The future of our understanding of God needs to keep the dual dimensions of immanent and transcendent relationships between the ultimate and the human, so that we can freely go back and forth between the two images, the supreme God and the inmost Self.

To put it more concretely I think what the Christian presence in East Asia today can offer is in the following areas. First is the dual concept of grace understood as both a universal grace (the imprint of *imago Dei*) and a special charism given to a few in order to make all beings achieve their original state as intended by the Creator. In other words, while the whole cosmos is to be graced, a special grace is given to particular persons as a means to help the universal call. Thus, the Christian emphasis on grace can be a living token and challenge to other religious systems of thought by recalling this dimension in their own traditions and viewing the total reality of this world from the light above. If we keep the relationship between the ultimate and humanity alive by the notion of grace, ordinary human life and the total natural world will reflect a divine light that gives a purifying energy.

The second area where the Christian presence can help in contemporary East Asia is closely connected to the first. It is in the Christian appreciation of the value of the individual human person and the democratic process of political organizations and decision making. Among the native schools of thought in East Asia, it was Taoism that upheld the equality of all beings and the freedom of individuals. The mythic character of Taoism which saw a utopia in the realm of the immortals, however, hindered concretizing its spirit into various human organizations so as to develop a truly democratic style of government in families, religious orders, and societies. But this longing for economic equity, egalitarian evaluation of all beings, and the ideal of a small com-

---

[11] Julia Ching, *Confucianism and Christianity: A Comparative Study* (Kodansha, 1977).

munity where people can live naturally and simply has lingered on and been kept alive by Taoist thinkers. Christians should support this longing and work together by offering concrete democratic processes in every level of community. A truly egalitarian community will be a fulfillment of this longing as well as a stepping stone to the kingdom of God, where all human discriminations disappear.

The third area where the Christian presence can help is witnessing the value and redemptive power of the cross through honest dialogue. Both Confucianism and Taoism have known the value of suffering that comes from overcoming oneself, but their fundamental outlook on human nature and the natural world was an optimistic one. The outlook of folk religious culture such as Shamanism or Shinto was also basically positive without a sharp distinction between good and evil, real and unreal. It was Buddhism introduced from Indian spiritual soil that perceived the phenomenal world as something passing and all human attachments as the cause of suffering. It is ignorance—not seeing things as they are, that they are in fact empty in themselves and interdependent on each other for their own existence—that causes the cycles of life. Buddhism shares with Christianity its basic negative outlook toward the present situation in which we are living. Buddhism teaches the way of enlightenment from ignorance, while Christianity shows the way of salvation through the cross and resurrection. Enlightenment shows us how to see reality as it is, while salvation offers spiritual power to carry the cross. The former opens up the eye of mind, while the latter energizes and stirs the love of the heart. It is true that full enlightenment brings forth the energy to be merciful and the experience of salvation also offers a vision of life. But it is also true that through dialogue we learn to see each other's strength and also be strengthened by the other's challenge.

I have been involved in interreligious dialogue for the past ten years. Along with small academic discussions four times a year, we have offered ten monthly lectures for religious on a specific topic each year. At the present time we have finished six series of lectures and discussions on Zen Buddhism and Christianity, Religious Life in Christianity and Buddhism, Christianity and Korean Shamanism, Social Spirituality of Confucianism and Christianity, Taoism and Christianity, and New Korean Religions and Christianity. These dialogue experiences have taught me that not only am I being stimulated to grasp the true picture of Christianity, but my partners in dialogue are also challenged to be transparent and recover their own original images. Naturally I was quite sympathetic when I read the report from the Asian Bishops' Synod in 1999.[12] The threefold dialogue—that is, interreligious dialogue, dialogue with one's own culture, and dialogue with the marginalized—is definitely the most urgent task ahead for us in this century. These threefold dialogues are closely connected, for the basic spirit of each of them is mutual respect that values the rights of identity and autonomy in its full sense. The marginalized are to be self-supportive; our own culture should be accepted and transformed with the Christian experience of grace; and our neighbor's religions are to be respected and appreciated.

Conclusion

What does it mean, then, to be a missionary community, and what is the mission for the Christians in the twenty-first century? Monika Hellwig defines mission thus: "In its general sense mission refers to the sending of someone to do something on behalf of another."[13] In the Christian context, God is the ultimate agent who sends people to carry out the divine command; people who have been missioned are Abraham, Moses, prophets, and above all Jesus. Jesus sent his disciples, his church community, to do his work, that is, to proclaim the good news that the kingdom of God is coming among us.

The kingdom of God is like yeast, an energy-filled grace to transform our distorted relational existence into an equitable, sharing, and respectful society as the story of Zacchaeus portrays (Luke 19:8-10) so well. In the Confucian context, heaven is the ultimate agent to bestow the dual command: one command to every human person to become a benevolent man/woman; another command to particular persons, and especially the polit-

---

[12] John Mansford Prior, S.V.D., "Apostles and Martyrs: Consecrated Life at the Bishop's Synod for Asia," *Review for Religious* 58 (Jan.-Feb. 1999): 27.

[13] *The Modern Catholic Encyclopedia* (Collegeville, Minn.: Liturgical Press, 1994), 575.

ical leaders, to teach people and to form a benevolent society. In the Taoist context, the Tao is the ultimate teacher to call forth the sages who follow the way of Tao, so that a natural harmony may be established not only in human communities but also within the total cosmos. Therefore, when we look more deeply, every human person and every cultural community has a sense of mission from above.

Then what is the unique mission of the Christian communities in East Asia today? I will try to state again the three points, drawing directly from the recently published *Ecclesia in Asia*, the Holy Father's Apostolic Exhortation on the church in Asia (November 6, 1999). My choice and emphasis might be subjective, but I feel the following three points are crucial for the future of the Christian presence.

1. Christian communities as well as individuals, especially the spiritual leaders, have to witness human warmth and maturity as the living signs of a merciful Jesus and his Father. *Ecclesia in Asia* states, "The Second Vatican Council taught clearly that the entire Church is missionary, and that the work of evangelization is the duty of the whole People of God" (art. 42). It also quotes the following Propositio 8 of the Synod Fathers: "The Good News of Jesus Christ can only be proclaimed by those who are taken up and inspired by the love of the Father for his children, manifested in the person of Jesus Christ. This proclamation is a mission needing holy men and women who will make the Saviour known and loved through their lives. A fire can only be lit by something that is itself on fire" (art. 23). In East Asia academic learning or theory has been valued only as far as it helps practical living and formation of the mature personality. Therefore, the love of God and neighbor in preaching only is an empty sound that does not carry the power to persuade people, let alone gain any respect of other religious practitioners. It is a loving and benevolent person who speaks. A Christian person who undergoes suffering in order to restore justice to people is the living witness who carries on the mission of Christianity, for the power of the cross and vitality of grace are vividly exhibited in his/her life.

2. The Christian churches have to be praying communities who truly seek the will of God and constantly purify both their hearts and their activities in order to be transparent witnesses.

Ecclesia in Asia states: "Mission is contemplative action and active contemplation. Therefore, a missionary who has no deep experience of God in prayer and contemplation will have little spiritual influence or missionary success" (art. 23). Since the work of justice and charity is easily corrupted without a purifying effect of prayer, it is not overstated that the future of the mission depends to a great extent on contemplation. This is true in Christian churches everywhere, but it is more so in East Asia, for it is the quality of spirituality that is the norm of judgment to prove or disprove the validity of Christian presence. It is, therefore, interesting that the pope strongly encourages the establishment of monastic and contemplative communities wherever possible.[14] Even the active religious congregations are beginning to feel the need to strengthen their spirituality and to try to build the house of silence for their members, so that they can spend an extended period of time solely to experience the presence of God. This trend will probably spread out even to the laity, so that the total congregation will be inflamed by the Spirit of God. Moreover, if this purifying effect of contemplation leads us to form egalitarian communities where individual dignity is respected, the Christian witness will be truly attractive.

3. The dialogue with one's own traditional culture and other religious traditions has to be the fundamental requirement for Christians in Asia in order to be effective witnesses. *Ecclesia in Asia* states:

> The desire for dialogue, however, is not simply a strategy for peaceful coexistence among peoples; it is an essential part of the Church's mission because it has its origin in the Father's loving dialogue of salvation with humanity through the Son in the power of the Holy Spirit. . . . The dialogue which the Church proposes is grounded in the logic of the Incarnation. Therefore, nothing but fervent and unselfish solidarity

---

[14] John Paul II, *Ecclesia in Asia*, November 6, 1999, art. 44; English text p. 41. He recommends to religious in Asia: "The search for God, a life of fraternal communion, and service to others are the three chief characteristics of the consecrated life which can offer an appealing Christian testimony to the peoples of Asia today."

prompts the Church's dialogue with the men and women of
Asia who seek the truth in love. (art. 29)

Sometimes what we forget is the fact that in order to carry on the
dialogue fervently, we need to invest time, energy, and our best
people to learn other religions and cultural traditions adequately.
In many seminaries and religious formation houses we do not sin-
cerely allow time and personnel to prepare a good interreligious
dialogue. The result is quite clear. Our understanding of our own
cultural heritage is shallow and our dialogue is generally superficial with a deep-seated fear that we might lose our identity or our
young members. Truth should make us free, and our dialogue
should touch the bottom of our existence to the extent that both
sides are open to grace for mutual transformation.

The very concept of "mission" will be transformed when we
accept not only a Christian understanding of it but also the Confucian concept of the mission of life as Heaven's Mandate to form
a benevolent person and society, as well as the Taoist concept of
mission to follow the way of non-action so that every being and
every community celebrate self-transformation. We will respect
each other as dignified human beings and human communities
who treasure a clear mission in life. Since one God has created all
humanity, and one Holy Spirit has graced us to live self-tran-
scending lives, we have to have confidence that the Spirit of God
will lead us to the various images of the divine Son crucified and
glorified.

Response to Sung-Hae Kim

Michael Amaladoss, S.J.

I CONGRATULATE SISTER SUNG-HAE KIM FOR HER PRESENTATION. Following Confucian thought, she has shown how God reaches out to all but also how God may call some individuals for particular tasks in the service of mission. Taoism helped her to point to the transformative and social dimension of mission. Reflecting on the experience of Christians in Japan, China, and Korea, Sr. Kim then went on to stress the importance of dialogue. While appreciating and supporting the reflections and proposals of Sr. Kim, I would like, in this response, to underline and to continue reflecting on three of the points that she has made in her presentation.

Is Our Situation One of Original Blessing or Original Curse?

Asian traditions such as the Confucian and the Taoist, but also the Hindu and the Buddhist, affirm the basic goodness of humans and of the world. Not that they are ignorant of weakness and even evil, especially in the form of egoism and desire. But they view human beings as free and capable of self-transformation. This view gives rise to a certain basic trust in humans as creators of their own future. This positive view contrasts with the traditional way in which Christians look at themselves and the world. Thanks to original sin humans are weak and sinful or evil. The world too is affected by this evil. Humans cannot get out of this situation on their own. There is a basic distrust of humans; they need a savior. The outlook is, on the whole, pessimistic.

This pessimism is strengthened by a dichotomy that radically differentiates creatures from their Creator. Humans are *merely* humans, and God is an outsider to the sinful human world, coming as Savior to help people who cannot help themselves. In the Asian religious traditions there is not such a radical dichotomy between the divine and the human. Taoism and Advaitic Hinduism speak of the divine in the human. When they speak of the goodness and the capacity of humans, they refer not to the merely human of the Western and Christian tradition, but rather to the human whose rootedness in the divine is never radically broken even by sin. God, the indweller in the human heart, does not disappear when humans sin, but continues as the voice of conscience, calling them to conversion and enabling them from within to transform themselves. Redemption is not a rescue operation from without, but a recreation from within. Salvation is not a commercial operation to be negotiated through indulgences, but a reappropriation of the divine-in-the-human that has been tarnished by sin. In the face of transgression, shame rather than guilt is the predominant emotion in Confucianism.

Today we talk about humans being in the image of God and their inalienable dignity, which they do not lose even when they are sinners. Asian anthropology will support and further deepen these perspectives. It will also help us refocus our goals in mission as helpers in the ongoing divine–human dialogue that starts with creation in every human heart and religion.

Asian Churches

Talking of the church in Korea, Sr. Kim remarks that, while the church is at the center of society in the political and the economical fields, it is at the margins culturally. In other Asian countries, except the Philippines, the church will be at the margins also economically and politically. The lessons of Matteo Ricci and Roberto de Nobili have not been learned. The churches in Asia are seen as foreign implants that depend on power centers abroad politically, financially, ideologically, and culturally.

During the special Synod for Asia there were some mild voices that claimed a rightful autonomy for the local churches of Asia. These voices were effectively silenced. The church's mission in Asia is perceived by many to be something organized, directed, and financed from outside. At an international mission congress in Manila in 1979 it was affirmed that every local church is on mission in its own territory and collaborates with other local churches in universal mission. This vision may have been realized with regard to personnel in many Asian countries, thanks to restrictive immigration policies of many Asian governments. But ideologically and organizationally we are still dependent. Christians themselves may feel foreign in the local sociocultural context.

It is in this context that we need to enter into dialogue with the three-self model of the Chinese church, without any detriment to the reality of the universal church as the communion of local churches. We have to explore what are the real conditions and demands of such communion. There seems to be a lack of clarity even in terminology. Should we talk about Asian churches or about the church in Asia?

At the moment, inculturation is still being pushed as the translation of the current ecclesial structures in various cultural forms and not as the creative response to the gospel of various peoples in terms of their own cultural symbols and structures. We do not seem to realize that the witness of the Asian churches to the kingdom will be authentic and effective only when they are really and totally indigenous. This is the principle of the incarnational economy: real transformation in Jesus and in the Spirit is from within.

The only areas in which the Asian Christians felt a little free to explore and express themselves were spirituality and theological reflection. But there are increasing attempts to impose uniformity even in these areas.

Becoming Empty

In the context of Taoism, Sr. Kim suggests the need for emptiness and humility. She contrasts this with the aggression, oppression, and even destruction that have characterized Christian mission in the past.

When the Word of God became human, it emptied itself and became a servant, though God made him Lord. Today we skip the phase of emptiness and claim the fullness that is the Lord's and that will be ours—that is, everyone's—only on the last day.

Our mission aims at fulfilling everyone else—other religions and cultures. We no longer have the political power to support this project, but we still seem to believe in economic and media power. We claim for ourselves the power of the Spirit. We have started speaking the language of rights. Recently the church asked pardon for many of its deeds in the past. But this humility does not seem to affect its pretensions when it comes to mission. Too many feel that we Christians have nothing to receive or learn from anyone.

We need to explore whether this is the appropriate mind-set with which to go on mission. First of all, mission is primarily God's mission: God sending God's Word and God's Spirit to communicate God's desire to be with humanity. This is the universal economy of which Sr. Kim also speaks. This is also affirmed by *Ad Gentes*. This is prior to any particular vocation—that of the church, for example. We cannot therefore think of our action in mission without taking into account what God has been doing everywhere long before we reach anywhere. Second, the fact that God calls someone for a special task in the context of God's mission does not make him/her a plenipotentiary representative of God. Yet this is the status we seem to claim in the name of Jesus. Jesus proclaimed the kingdom. Today we seem to proclaim the church, without seeing any difference.

The Asian perspective of emptiness, which we find in Taoism, as Sr. Kim has shown, and which is even stronger in Buddhism, can help us to be open to be filled by God, free of our egoism, attachments, and pride. Such an attitude will also make us more ready for real dialogue, where we are as open to receive from others as to give and share our God-experience.

Finally, I agree with Sr. Kim that mission in the third millennium will be dialogic. Dialogue is also the Asian way, as the bishops of Asia affirmed at a recent assembly of the Federation of Asian Bishops' Conferences (FABC) in Thailand in January 2000. If we need a good lesson in dialogue, let us dialogue with the Confucian and Taoist traditions from East Asia.

2

Identity and Harmony

Challenges to Mission in South Asia

Michael Amaladoss, S.J.

IN SOUTH ASIA, THE PLURALISM OF RELIGIONS IS NOT MERELY a fact; it is also a problem. Religious groups are in conflict. In India, Hindu–Muslim riots have been going on for more than seventy years. Recently, Hindu fundamentalists have started attacking Christians. In Pakistan and Bangladesh, most Hindus have migrated. Antiblasphemy laws seem to target Christians in Pakistan. With a few reserved seats in parliament, they are not an integral part of political life there. In Sri Lanka the ongoing civil war has both ethnic and religious dimensions. In Burma the conflict of the government with the Karen rebels also has both ethnic and religious roots.

Religious identity is certainly a factor in these conflicts, but the conflicts themselves have political roots. Analysts point out that these conflicts seem to emerge when a country passes from an authoritarian to a democratic political order. Under colonial or strong governments, often supported by the military forces, different ethnic and religious groups live together under domination. But when these authoritarian orders collapse, there is competition for power. The majority groups try to assert their dominance because of their numbers. The minority groups seek to protect themselves and search for autonomy. The political struggle itself may be inspired by economic factors: which group enjoys the economic benefits of being in control, especially in a situation of scarce resources in poor countries, where there is not enough to meet the needs of everyone—to say nothing of the greed of some. Groups can coalesce around many factors: caste, ethnicity, culture, language, or religion.

Very often the power of religious identity is used by economic and political forces for their own ends. In South Asia we call this *communalism*. This is opposed to *fundamentalism*. Fundamentalists are people who believe that the fundamental perspectives on which their religion is based are true as against the fundamentals of other religions, which are false. They seek to impose their truth on others, provoking self-defensive reactions from them. This conflict is purely at the religious level, though sometimes the fundamentalists may be supported by political power. Religions therefore can be causes for social conflict, either because they are fundamentalistic or communalistic or both.

The potential that religion has for such conflicts consists in the sense of social identity and integration that it confers on a particular group. It is necessary to understand this if we want to grasp the reality and force of interreligious conflicts and explore ways of resolving them.

Religion and Identity

The self or identity of a person is shaped by the mental representation that the person has not only of one's bodily life and of primary relationships within one's family but also of one's culture and its configuration of beliefs about humans, nature, and the others, including the Other. These representations are transmitted and interiorized through symbols and rituals. In the early years of childhood, just as the child develops the sense of "I am!" in opposition to another, it also develops a sense of "We are!" in opposition to other groups who share the cognitive and physical space with one's own community. Cognitive psychologists suggest that "the mere perception of two different groups is sufficient to trigger a positive evaluation of one's own group and a negative stereotyping of the other."[1] Sudhir Kakar, an Indian psychoanalyst, explains how this stereotyping occurs in childhood.

Because of early difficulties in integrating contradictory representations of the self and the parents—the "good" loving child and the "bad" raging one; the good, care-taking parent and the hateful, frustrating one—the child tries to disown the bad representations through projection. First projected to inanimate objects and animals and later to people and other groups—the latter often available to the child as a preselection by the group—the disavowed bad representations *need* such "reservoirs." . . . These reservoirs—Muslims for Hindus, Arabs for Jews, Tibetans for the Chinese, and vice versa—are also convenient repositories for subsequent rages and hateful feelings for which no clear-cut addressee is available. Since most of the "bad" representations arise from a social disapproval of the child's "animality," as expressed in its aggressivity, dirtiness, and unruly sexuality, it is preeminently this animality which a civilized, moral self must disavow and place in the reservoir group.[2]

The development of religious identity, both as personal and as group, seems to follow the same process as other group identities. The only difference is that the religious identity is much deeper because it has to do with the ultimate perspectives of meaning, goals, and motivations in life. Kakar says:

The involvement of religious rather than other social identities does not dampen but, on the contrary, increases the violence of the conflict. Religion brings to conflict between groups a greater emotional intensity and a deeper motivational thrust than language, region or other markers of ethnic identity.[3]

---

[1] Sudhir Kakar, *The Colors of Violence: Cultural Identities, Religion, and Conflict* (Chicago: University of Chicago Press, 1996), 243.

[2] Ibid., 243-44.

[3] Ibid., 247.

Identity and Community

It would be convenient if different religious groups lived in different geographical areas, as, for example, Samuel Huntington would wish.[4] Even then conflict cannot be avoided, because one group will try to dominate the globe. The reality is that in most parts of the world—and especially in South Asia—we are living in religiously pluralistic communities. Can we live in peace or are we condemned to perpetual conflict? What sort of community can we create in a multireligious situation? Two kinds of solutions have been tried in South Asia.

We have countries such as Pakistan, whose *raison d'être* is religious identity. Islam is the official religion of the state. The believers of other religions are tolerated but reduced to second-class status. They may also be persecuted in various ways. We cannot talk of a community here. Sri Lanka and Burma give a special place to Buddhism; Nepal used to be a Hindu kingdom.

India established a secular republic, which respects religious freedom. The state is not merely a-religious or neutral, but positive toward religions. The religious minorities are even specially protected. From the beginning, this secularism was understood in two ways. Some sought to privatize religion and thought that, with the development of science and technology, religion would really become irrelevant in course of time. Others thought that secularism meant that all religions must play an equal role in public life and that the state itself must not favor any one religion, but should encourage all religions equally. The tension between these two views continues, though I think that the second view is now slowly gaining ground.[5] According to this view the state must be neutral with regard to religion. But in public life the different religions must be recognized, accepted, respected, and enabled to make their special contribution toward the well-being

---

[4] Samuel P. Huntington, *The Clash of Civilizations and the Remaking of World Order* (London: Touchstone Books, 1997).

[5] See T. N. Madan, *Modern Myths, Locked Minds: Secularism and Fundamentalism in India* (Delhi: Oxford University Press, 1996); Ashis Nandy, "The Politics of Secularism and the Recovery of Religious Tolerance," in *Mirrors of Violence,* ed. Veena Das (Delhi: Oxford University Press, 1990).

of the community. Through conversation, discussion, and even controversy, the various religious groups must seek a consensus that will guide public policy. We have to move toward a new kind of democratic order that is dominated by a majority but is participative, allowing every group, large and small, to make its proper contribution to the common good. This way of thinking is very similar to the discussions on multiculturalism in North America.[6]

Such an approach to the role of religion in public life supposes a particular way of looking at religion. It is not ignorance and superstition that are destined to disappear with the advance of modern science and technology. It does not make a fundamentalist claim to give a total and exhaustive meaning to life. It recognizes the autonomy of the secular sphere of economics, politics, and society, but it does offer an ultimate perspective on everything. Religions, in their effort to be relevant to society, may tend to legitimate existing social structures, offering them ultimate justification. But religions, because they deal with ultimate perspectives, are capable of being self-critical and also countercultural with regard to society, challenging it to change. It is at this level that religions can collaborate to provide a common moral and spiritual foundation to the sociopolitical and economic order.

This is the multireligious context that challenges Christians in mission in South Asia. Christians are part of this context. They are small minorities in the South Asian countries, but their reading of the challenges will depend on their idea of mission in a multireligious context.

The Church and Other Religions

The attitude of the church to other religions has carried with it an *a priori* judgment about their status. The church claims fullness of revelation and fullness of the means of salvation. From this high ground it looks at other religions. In the course of the last fifty years, the church's view of other religions has undergone

---

[6] See *Multiculturalism,* ed. Amy Gutmann (Princeton: Princeton University Press, 1994); and *Theorizing Multiculturalism,* ed. Cynthia Willett (Oxford: Blackwell, 1998).

many changes. Before the Second Vatican Council the church had a negative view of other religions, though it accepted the possibility of individual salvation in one way or another. At the council, the church accepted some good and holy elements or the "seeds of the Word" in other religions. Even when it defended the freedom of people to follow the religion of their choice, this was done in the name of the dignity of the human person created in the image of God, and not in terms of any worth attributed to the religions themselves. Even in the apostolic exhortation *Evangelii Nuntiandi*, other religions were compared to the hands outstretched to heaven to which the Christian revelation came as a response. In 1986, by inviting the leaders of other religions to come together at Assisi to pray for peace in the world, John Paul II acknowledged the legitimacy of other religions—that they can mediate divine–human relationship in prayer that is therefore effective. In 1990, in *Redemptoris Missio*, the pope affirms that the Spirit of God is present and active in other religions. Other religions are still compared to the church as preparation to fulfillment, and the church is said to be the ordinary way to salvation.

This is a strange history. We Christians, of course, are happy to see that the church has become increasingly positive toward other religions. But members of other religions probably question the perspective, the method, and the criteria as well as the credibility of a theology that has turned 180 degrees from a negative view of their religions to a positive view that accepts other religions as "extraordinary" ways to the divine. Some adherents of other religions resent the patronizing and condescending tone directed toward them, especially after we say that we respect their freedom as human beings and the freedom of the Spirit of God present and active in them. If we really believe that the Spirit of God is active in them and we respect their freedom, then it is not proper for us to claim the right to judge them, using our experience of God as a criterion. I think that such a theology of other religions needs more than a few minor corrections. We need to try a new approach.

A New Approach

This new approach should not be *a priori,* but should start from the reality and experience of other religions, that is to say, from an *a posteriori* approach. Starting with creation, the Spirit of God has been active in the world, in human beings, and in their religions. The human conscience has been the voice of the divine, guiding people, and they have been freely responding to God in their lives. God has also been speaking to various people through many prophets and sages (Heb. 1:1). This divine–human relationship is salvific. The salvation to which God calls everyone is not an escape of individuals from hellfire into heaven. Salvation is a call to fullness that starts already in this life (Luke 4:16-18) but achieves its consummation on the last day. An important element of this fullness is the communitarian dimension of universal reconciliation and unity when God will be "all in all" (1 Cor. 15:28). This is the kingdom that is God's gift to humanity and also our task. This plan of God for the universe is rooted in creation, achieved in the paschal mystery and consummated with the second coming of Christ, when the whole of humanity will be gathered together (Matt. 25). All the religions are players in this historical movement, which is orchestrated by the Spirit of God. This is God's own—the Father, Word, and Spirit—mission, according to *Ad Gentes* 2. John Paul II affirms the unity of the plan of God very strongly.

> There is *only one* divine plan for every human being who comes into this world (Jn 1:9), one single origin and goal, whatever may be the color of his skin, the historical and geographical framework within which he happens to live and act, or the culture in which he grows up and expresses himself. The differences are a less important element, when confronted with the unity which is radical, fundamental, and decisive. . . . If it is the order of unity that goes back to creation and redemption and is therefore, in this sense, "divine," such differences—and even religious divergences —go back rather to a "human" fact, and must be overcome in progress towards the realization of the mighty plan of unity which dominates the creation.[7]

It is in the context of this plan of God, which spans the whole of human history, that we must set the call to particular individ-

---

[7] Address to cardinals before Christmas 1986, reported in *Pontifical Council for Interreligious Dialogue Bulletin* 22 (1987): 55-57.

uals and to groups. The kingdom of God is the horizon in which the plan of God is being realized. The church, as the body of the disciples of Jesus, is called to be the "sacrament" according to *Lumen Gentium* 1, that is to say, symbol and servant of the kingdom of God. The church is missioned to build the kingdom, not itself, except as its symbol and servant.

Other Religions as Collaborators

Jesus proclaimed the kingdom as a human community of freedom and fellowship, justice and love. He inaugurated it, and it is being realized in a tensive dynamic of "already–not yet." The forces opposed to the kingdom are the egoistic and exploitative structures of Satan and Mammon. Jesus wanted the people to turn from these evil and sinful forces to God. It is from these oppressive powers that Jesus liberated the people. Other religions too are opposed to these forces of evil. But by some quirk of history mission became a campaign not against Satan and Mammon but against other religions. Often the other religions were seen as the works of Satan. Conversion was seen as turning away not primarily from the evil powers of Satan but from other religions. As a matter of fact, the other religions are also opposed to the sinful forces of Satan and Mammon. In promoting the kingdom, then, our enemies are Satan and Mammon, not other religions. The other religions are rather our allies. As John Paul II told the leaders of other religions whom he met in Chennai, India, in February 1986: "As followers of different religions we should join together in promoting and defending common ideals in the spheres of religious liberty, human brotherhood, education, culture, social welfare and civic order."[8]

In his encyclical *Sollicitudo Rei Socialis*, John Paul II refers to the prayer meeting in Assisi, October 1986:

The meeting held on 27 October last in Assisi, the city of St. Francis, in order to pray for and commit ourselves to *peace*

---

[8] John Paul II, in *Origins* 15 (1986): 598.

—each one in fidelity to his own religious profession—
showed how much *peace* and, as its necessary condition, the
development of the whole person and of all peoples, are also
a *matter of religion,* and how the full achievement of both
the one and the other depends on our *fidelity* to our vocation as men and women of faith. For it depends, above all,
on God. (par. 47)

The religions then, are our allies, in our pursuit of the kingdom
of God.

One of the problems that might cloud our point of view in this
area is the easy identification of the church with the kingdom.
The church is not the kingdom; it is its symbol and servant. The
kingdom is an eschatological reality whose full realization is in
the future. The church itself, together with other religions, is in
pilgrimage toward the kingdom. If the kingdom is where God is
present and active, then it is also present in other religions and in
all people of good will. In Jesus' self-manifestation there was a
strong kenotic principle (Phil. 2:7). The church seems to have
turned it into a triumphalistic one. Jesus proclaimed the kingdom
of God. The early church proclaimed Christ. The later church
proclaimed itself. This evolution is taken as normal, but it could
be questioned. Though Jesus was divine, he emptied himself and
became a human being, limited by his human nature, culture, and
history. The church's reception of this kenotic revelation is
affected by the same human, cultural, and historical condition-
ing, to which should be added its sinfulness. Yet it does not hesi-
tate to attribute to itself a fullness that is proper only to the
divine-human Jesus. I think that the church will be more ready to
collaborate with other religions if it is aware of its limitations. It
will also be more ready to learn from others.

What is the specific task of the church in mission? It is called
to be the symbol of the kingdom. It is also called to be at its service. In this it will follow the way of Jesus: of humility, of selfless,
sacrificial love unto death, of the option for the poor and the
marginalized, of assurance founded on its experience of the risen
Jesus and of the Spirit. I think that the church is called also in a
special way to promote God's plan of universal reconciliation
revealed to it in Jesus (Eph. 1:1-10).

Harmony and Dialogue

The Christians in Asia, starting from their experience of religious and other pluralisms, have contextualized this vision of mission in terms of a goal and a way. They are harmony and dialogue. When we think of unity, we normally tend to think in terms of uniformity. From a conceptual, logical point of view, unity cannot tolerate difference. If a certain pluralism is really inescapable, then unity is thought of in terms of a hierarchical structure. In Asia, both in the Chinese and in the Indian cultural traditions, there is a perspective of holism and harmony that accepts and respects difference and looks upon pluralism as richness. The *yin* and the *yang* of the Chinese tradition seek harmony in dynamic movement. The images of the peaceful sitting Buddha and the dancing *Nataraja* are Indian expressions of harmony that manifest an Absolute that is inclusive and integrating. The Tibetan *mandalas* are meditative instruments for producing inner harmony. This harmony is experienced at the level of the person through holistic methods of *sadhana* such as the yoga. In society right relationships and consideration for others are stressed. Harmony with the cosmos is also promoted in terms of symbols and rituals, particularly music. The Ultimate is experienced not as the dominating Other but as the indweller who sustains and integrates everything.

Such harmony in life, community, and cosmos can be achieved only through collaboration and dialogue. The reference here is not to interreligious dialogue, but to a basic way of life and relationship that is born of a profound respect for the other, who is free and different. Dialogue is a way of acknowledging and accepting the other's identity shown in the readiness to listen, to change, and to collaborate. The themes of harmony and dialogue come back in various documents of Asian bishops and theologians. Here is an example:

Jesus Christ is continuing his Spirit-filled mission of restoring peace and harmony with God and among humans. . . . his disciples are called to be effective signs of union with God and unity of humankind. . . . In them, the attitude of harmony is to become a Christian attitude of respect for mother Earth. . . . They are, with open mind and a humble heart, to recognize in all sisters and brothers, of whatever faith-conviction and culture, fellow wayfarers to God's Reign. It is through triple dialogue with cultures, with religions and with the poor, through a mutually-enriching interchange in its various modes and at various levels, not the least in the dialogue of life with people of other faiths and religious traditions, that Asian Christianity is to strive for human and cosmic harmony in Jesus Christ.[9]

At their assembly in January 2000, the Federation of Asian Bishops' Conferences (FABC) sought to discern an Asian way of fulfilling the church's mission of love and service.

We are committed to the emergence of the Asian-ness of the Church in Asia. This means that the Church has to be an embodiment of the Asian vision and values of life, especially: interiority, harmony, a holistic and inclusive approach to every area of life. . . . We believe in the innate spiritual insight and moral wisdom in the Asian soul; and it is the core around which a growing sense of "being Asian" is built. This "being Asian" is best discovered and affirmed, not in confrontation and opposition, but in the spirit of complementarity and harmony.[10]

Peacemakers

In a situation of interreligious conflict, our first task is conflict resolution or peacemaking. We have seen that it is not only religion that causes conflict. The reasons may be economic, political, or social, and these causes have to be identified and addressed.

---

[9] See the document "Asian Christian Perspectives on Harmony," in *For All the Peoples of Asia*, vol. 2, ed. Franz-Josef Eilers, S.V.D. (Manila: Claretian Press, 1997), 285-86.

[10] "A Renewed Church in Asia: A Mission of Love and Service" (The final statement of the 7th plenary assembly of the Federation of Asian Bishops' Conferences, Samphar, Thailand, January 3-12, 2000), Part 3, "The Challenge of Discerning the Asian Way."

We cannot have peace without justice and equality. It may often be a question of fears rather than facts; we need authoritative voices that assuage the fears and clarify the doubts. Other reasons for conflict may be ignorance and prejudice, past hurts and suspicions. Knowledge can remove ignorance, and the possibility of living contact and conversation can clear prejudice. A healing process involving forgiving and forgetting may be necessary to get over hurts. All these can be done in a planned manner. Symbolic gestures at the level of leadership may be very helpful to reassure people at other levels. Sometimes peace committees are set up during communal riots. Sociologists speak of "institutionalized riot systems" that take advantage of any critical incident.[11] These could be countered by "institutionalized peace committees."

Not only can conflicts be resolved; they can be prevented, if we build up multireligious action groups that are committed to struggle for equality and justice with a special option for the poor, the marginalized, the oppressed, and the minorities. They can also promote common human and spiritual values, defend human rights, and encourage solidarity. Narrow group identities can be transcended only by identifying with larger groups. Asian theologians have spoken of the need to build up Basic Human Communities in Asia that will necessarily be multireligious. While information may provide knowledge, the removal of prejudice and of emotional blocks is possible only when people experience solidarity in common struggle and collaboration.

Interreligious Dialogue

It is in the context of such a collaboration in the building up of the kingdom of God that dialogue between religions at a religious level becomes meaningful. We can think of various dimensions of such dialogue. In working together for the promotion of common human and spiritual values, each religious group finds justification for its participation in its own religious resources. At this

---

[11] See Paul R. Brass, *Theft of an Idol: Text and Context in the Representation of Collective Violence* (Calcutta: Seagull Books, 1998), 210-11.

stage, coming from different directions, the group tries to work toward a consensus on common objectives and actions. At a second stage, the believers of different religions can share their faith perspectives in a prophetic context, challenging each other to change when necessary, and listening and being enriched. The effort here is not comparative study of doctrines, nor is it to find some common ground that can support collaboration. The identity and difference of the other are respected, but one lets oneself be challenged by what is different. One can hope for a slow convergence of views and perspectives. At some stage of this convergence, common prayer may become meaningful. In India we have the Gandhian tradition of common prayer in the service of communal peace. People come together to listen to readings from different Scriptures, sing bhajans and share prayer.

Obstacles

From the side of the Christians we can speak of three kinds of obstacles to promoting interreligious collaboration and harmony. Collaboration presupposes that the different religious groups feel a basic common bond as members of one national community, for instance. Unfortunately, we are still considered foreign. We ourselves feel that we are not still really a local church. There has been a lot of talk about inculturation after the Second Vatican Council. But not only are any real efforts toward inculturation being blocked; even the local leadership does not see it as a need, except for some exterior decor. Socially most of us live like Indians. But as soon as we cross the threshold of the church building our language, dress, gestures, and symbols take on foreign accents. Such foreignness is imposed as essential for authentic divine–human encounter. Economically we do not live within our means and so have to depend on foreign resources. Administratively, we are dependent on foreign centers of power. Feeble voices during the special Synod of Bishops for Asia demanding a certain autonomy were effectively ignored and silenced. When John Paul II visited India recently a group of Hindus said that he should come either as a head of state or as the head of a religion. We are ethnically Indians. Are we also Indians as Christians? Most of our institutions are purveyors of modernity identified as Western.

Some of the groups that become Christian may do so precisely in order to belong to a group that is not rooted in India but has international links. Unless we can shed this foreign image, dialogue will continue to be difficult. People may still be tolerant and relate to us, but as to a minority foreign group. In post-colonial countries there is a quest for and an assertion of national and cultural identity. In that context our position is ambiguous, perhaps even to many of us. When we do not have a clear identity, dialogue becomes a problem.

In recent years the opposition to conversion has been increasing. Gandhi represents a host of Hindus who will declare themselves disciples of Jesus Christ, but who will not become members of the church. The church reacts vehemently to this separation between itself and Jesus Christ, though the distinction is not totally baseless. But I do not think that the church has ever stopped to ask itself why people like Gandhi make such a distinction. Leaving one religion and joining another is never merely a religious change. It is also and always a social process. This is not to say that it is wrong as a social process. It may be a means of social protest. But it is good to recognize it as such and explore its consequences for social relationships. Today we have started to say that conversion is a human right, but in Asia there are no rights without corresponding duties and responsibilities. Dialogue starts right there, when we seek to understand and explain the legitimacy of such a process to ourselves and others. If we speak of the need to heal historical memories and hurts, then we cannot separate this question from memories of colonialism, whatever may have been the actual relationship between the churches and the colonizers.

A more strictly religious obstacle is that some of the literature we put out on evangelization may make others suspect that our commitment to dialogue is not wholehearted and that we seek to instrumentalize it for conversion. I wonder whether many of the Christians themselves are very clear about it. Asian bishops and theologians have developed over the years a particular way of talking about dialogue and evangelization. They speak about evangelization itself as a threefold dialogue with the poor, the rich cultures, and the great religions of Asia. If we respect the freedom of humans and the freedom of the Spirit of God active in them, then dialogue is the only way that we can talk to them about Jesus and his good news. But I wonder whether everyone is convinced about this. When Christians speak in many voices, we need not wonder if their motives are suspected by others.

Conclusion

Interreligious conflicts have become endemic in South Asia. They are not going to disappear for decades to come. In this context Christians in Asia are aware of their mission to promote harmony, which recognizes and respects the identity of every religious group and yet asserts that they can live together, because it is according to the plan of God for the world. A vision of harmony accepts multiple identities in the community as the gift of God for the enrichment of all. It promotes a participative democratic order to which every group has its contribution to make. It moves through consensus rather than through the domination by any one group. Dialogue is the appropriate way of promoting harmony. Any mission that is set in the context of the mission of God cannot but be dialogical. One of the obstacles that prevent Christians from playing their proper role in promoting harmony in South Asia is that they are not sure of their own identity and rootedness. May we hope that in the twenty-first century the churches in Asia will be able to become truly local churches, animated by a vision of harmony, in order to be credible servants of God's mission.

3

Three Cardinal Issues
of Mission in Africa

Mercy Amba Oduyoye

OF THE MANY ISSUES, CONCERNS, AND CHALLENGES OF God's mission through Christian witness in Africa, three are of particular interest to me—not that I am an expert on any of them, but these three impact my own life and those of persons that I have come to share my life with.

The first is the *relationship of Christians and Muslims*. Part of my extended family is Muslim, and for five years I lived in the midst of that line and continue that association through significant events. Let me say immediately that this in West Africa is no unique situation. An Anglican bishop and a Chief Imam could be womb-brothers in Africa. In the past ten years I have been a member of a multireligious Pan-African circle of African women theologians and through that have come to realize how deeply Muslim women yearn and work for their community to be an empowering one for women and for the development of Africa. Together we pray that God/Allah will save Africa from religious strife and put us on the path of peace.

The second issue is that of the *articulating of Christian theology* so that its relevance to Christian life-style becomes apparent. In this area, ecclesiology and Christology claim special attention. The latter has been the subject of academic discussion, while the former has claimed the attention of African women in theology.

It is Christology that this mission conference wishes to highlight and on which I shall therefore make two statements. The Christ-centered mission is anchored in a Christology of classical vintage —*Christus Victor*. Scanning christological writings from Africa that are being collected in anthologies such as Laurenti Magesa's and J. N. K. Mugami's 1989 volume *Jesus in African Christianity*, one is confronted with the reality captured by the title of another anthology, this one edited by Robert J. Schreiter, *Faces of Jesus in Africa*—there are many faces of Jesus in Africa. Anthologies generated by the Circle of Concerned African Women Theologians focus on what Jesus means in the lives of women and are a source for crafting Christology, as well as for discerning what African Christian women describe as a Christ-centered mission and ministry.

The third issue is *women and the gospel in Africa*. Given that two anthologies of African Women Theologians have taken as their theme the household of God, raising questions about the church's responsibility to be accountable to God for what happens to women, this is a most welcome task for me to undertake. I begin with what was chronologically the first mission challenge to surface on the African continent.

The Church and Islam in Africa

During the first millennium of the Christian era it was Mediterranean and Nilotic Africa that witnessed the encounter between Christianity and Islam. On the whole, with the exception of Ethiopia, Christianity was in retreat. As John Pobee has said, "The second millennium began with Christianity in disarray, fleeing before the Muslims and unsure of the future but determined to fight on."[1] European missionaries in Africa could not forget that between 634 and 644 C.E. African Christianity in the Mediterranean basin was replaced by Islam. Even more traumatic was the spread to Spain during the Umayyad period (661–

---

[1] See John S. Pobee, *AD 2000 and After: The Future of God's Mission in Africa* (Accra: Asempa Publishers, 1991).

749) and, as Pobee puts it, "the consternation generated by the gains of Islam in Southern Europe (1300-1500) struck fear and antipathy in the hearts of Europeans which they carried with them to Africa and made a part of the Christian culture" they propagated.

It was indeed the threat of Muslim Moors that caused Europe to launch into the evangelization of the rest of Africa from Cape Bojador to the Cape of Good Hope. It is a long story and seems a long time ago, but I suggest that the fear and mutual antipathy are barely hidden. It is a legacy of Christian missions, and response from Islam is evident. "The battle" has moved into Asia and Africa, areas where religion still counts for something. In West Africa, the religious riots of 1987 remain fresh memories. The Christian Association of Nigeria's Publicity Committee issued *A Catalogue of Events: For Posterity* showing burned churches and property of Christians. Rehearsing the history of conflicts we all know well is not my purpose here. Indeed, what we need to highlight are the pockets of good will, where women and men, Christian and Muslim are seeking the path of dialogue and mutual respect; that religion may not be a source of death but of life.

In 1960 a project to address this challenge was launched in Ibadan. It was at first named the "Islam in Africa Project," reflecting the European experience in the Iberian Peninsula. Later it was renamed ProCMuRA, "Project of Christian-Muslim Relations in Africa," an ecumenical effort begun in Ibadan, Nigeria, and now located in Nairobi, Kenya. This reflects the reality that Africa is pluralistic and that religious pluralism has to be acknowledged and lived in a creative manner and that Christians who did the launching into sub-Saharan Africa in a combative mood should take the initiative in promoting dialogue.

Dialogue with people of other religions, which in the early centuries of Christianity was known as apologetics, was effectively discredited by the utilization of the Augustinian dictum "compel them to come in." Instead of seeking and respecting dialogue partners, Western Christianity became violent and competitive, launching the theology of just war and aggressive mission "to compel" people to become Christians. Violence against those of religions other than Christianity was justified. But the Holy Spirit does lead us into all truth, and now led by Pope John Paul II we

Western Christians can recognize our part in inflicting suffering on others in the name of Christ.

It seems to me, then, that the way forward in respect to Islam is to promote ProCMuRA and similar organizations. The journal produced by this organization shows evidence of in-depth study. In order to illustrate the work of ProCMuRA I wish to refer readers to the following issues of their journal.

The May-June 1998 issue was a training course for ProCMuRA lay facilitators and carries articles on theological investigations. One contributor suggests that "[t]he Christological disagreements of the Council of Chalcedon need to be studied as a preliminary to taking on the Islamic objection to the Christian doctrine that Jesus is God." Further it is suggested that "[t]he Islamic doctrine of *Qadar* (predestination, fate) should not be taught to Christian students who do not know that at the Core of Calvin's theological system . . . stood the doctrine of predestination." The call for dialogue as mission is not a wishy-washy camaraderie. It includes careful sharing of theological insights— not comparison but a search for fuller understanding of the divine.

The July-August 1998 issue was dedicated to the life and mission of the church in relation to other faiths. Here it was stated that the essential thing in God's mission is to address the good news to all human beings in the context of their life experience. Since part of the experience is the religion one adheres to, mission becomes dialogue with people of living faiths with the aim of presenting the way and life of Jesus as the only manner to live a truly human life. Thus, becoming a member of a Christian church is not the *sine qua non* of one's response to the gospel.

Many Christians are shocked when Muslims demand slots on the national calendar of holidays. Having taken for granted Christian work-free days such as Sunday imposed on the whole nation at least in terms of closure of government institutions, we raise eyebrows when Muslims make similar demands. In March 1997, this question sparked political controversy in Mozambique. Dialogue calls for respecting your dialogue partner, and Christians in mission must honor this requirement.

There are efforts on several fronts to promote harmonious interreligious relations. Badru D. Kateregga and David W. Shenk have given us an example of "A Muslim and a Christian in Dialogue," in their book *Islam and Christianity*.[2] Modupe Oduyoye has prepared for ProCMuRA a short bibliography of published materials available to assist all those involved in the task of improving Christian–Muslim relations in Africa. The title is *The Churches' Responsibility for Understanding Islam and the Muslims in Africa*.[3] Some African Muslim women, especially Rabiatu Ammah of the Department for the Study of Religion, University of Ghana, have a ministry that includes helping all, Muslims and Christians alike, to clarify their understanding of Islam generally and specifically what the *Qur'an* says about women. Dr. Ammah has made several contributions to anthologies on this theme.[4]

As the first All-African Assembly of the Conferences on Religion and Peace in Nairobi in 1983 indicated, interreligious relations in Africa do not involve only Christianity and Islam. For Christians and Muslims, the first line of consideration is African religion. Conflicts have arisen out of confrontation of one or the other of the two Abrahamic faith communities with African religion. Both have to develop better approaches to adherents of this and other religions and their practices. At this meeting, Bishop Peter Sarpong, speaking on "Threats to Peace in Africa," named sin, especially pride, as the central threat to peace and a destroyer of justice, and the cause of lack of sensitivity to the other. What the bishop says about pride I suggest is applicable to the general attitude of Christians and Muslims toward the adherents of African religion. Pride, he says, "is that illusory sense of superiority whereby one regards all others, consciously or unconsciously as inferiors, even sub-human beings, unworthy of the rights one claims for oneself. Surely this cannot make for peace and mission has to evolve a strategy to evite this approach."[5]

---

[2] B. D. Kateregga and D. Shenk, *Islam and Christianity* (Nairobi: Uzima Press, 1980).

[3] M. A. Oduyoye, *The Churches' Responsibility for Understanding Islam and the Muslims in Africa* (Nairobi: ProCMuRA, 1995).

[4] Rabiatu Ammah, "Women in Islam" (extracts from a lecture given at the ProCMuRa Women's Conference, September 1993), *ProCMuRA* 3, no. 1 (January/February 1994): 5.

[5] Bishop Peter Sarpong, "Threats to Peace in Africa" (Religious Consideration, Africa Assembly of the Conferences on Religion and Peace, Nairobi, 1983).

As we review Islam in Africa as a traditional mission concern, the challenge I see is that we make an effort to understand in order to work to overcome the Christian fear of Islam that has fueled the mutual antipathy. Mission is about gospel, so we need to discern the good news not only as we know it in Christianity but also as it exists in the religion of "the other." Wherever this good news as read by Jesus in Nazareth is found, it is our Christian duty as people in God's mission to hail and to promote it.

We have entered an era in which Islam has become present in the Western world by trade and migration. This has been the case in Africa, Sudan, Nigeria, and the Gambia, where traders were the carriers for generations. Today television and globalization have made a reality the saying that for "Islam the world is a mosque." But just as Europe never forgot the era of forceful Islamization, so African churches are being reminded of the Utman dan Fodios and Samoras (1750-1900). The fact that this move was stopped by colonization is bringing Africans and some militant Western churches together to revive the fear of Islam. The situation is made volatile as militant Muslims claim the dan Fodio heritage. Mission in such an atmosphere demands prayer, wisdom, humility, openness, and sincerity.

A British rabbi, Julia Neuberger, assessing the religious scene on the brink of the new millennium, had this to say: "There are concerns about fundamentalism, of course, but this is a general issue for all religions, not just for Islam. If we see Islam becoming more fundamentalist, and Christianity more evangelical, then I do have worries that people will be more and more defined by faith. That would be dangerous."[6]

Women of Africa
and the Mission of the Gospel

Mission, I submit, is aimed at getting people to live the values of the gospel. Truly it is living the gospel that is the best test of the evangelization process. The past ten years and especially the

---

[6] In the *Cambridge Alumni Magazine* 26 (1999): 29.

last two have filled the ears of the world with two specifically Christian words, "evangelization" and "millennium." But have we filled the hungry with good things? The validity of the hunger of women for the respect due to their humanity is both questioned and dismissed. The term "millennium" is a periodization of world history with reference to Christ, and this should fill us with both joy and sorrow. Joy because the calendar we used to mark by B.C. and A.D. is now often referred to as before and since the beginning of the "Common Era." But sorrow is also appropriate, because the common era has largely remained words without deeds where women are concerned. As church we have been lethargic in our participation in the fulfillment of the mission of the gospel in Africa as far as it affects women.

In spite of this, the Roman Catholic Church in Africa has in recent years seen several African-originated women's religious congregations. Some were begun by church hierarchy; others by women themselves but supported by the church in accordance with established practice. In the whole church, women's organizations are the most visible at worship and the most dynamic in touching the lives of women. In Protestant and Charismatic churches, finances would collapse without the giving of women. And yet dealing with the hurts and visions of women remains on the level of verbal denunciation and palliative acts. We too often cry "Peace" where there is absence of *shalom*.

Working out their own salvation with fear and trembling, African Christian women have carried into the churches the strategy of segregating themselves in order to deal with the community challenges that they feel empowered to resolve, and where they cannot resolve problems they increasingly resort to public demonstration to draw attention to the threat. It is recognized by all who study the churches in Africa that women and women's groups are the most prominent in numerical terms. It is also clear from research that they are the ones drawn to prayer camps and special deliverance sessions because of the pains and agonies they have experienced.

Two Pan-African women's organizations whose activities are germane to the subject before us are the Pan-African Churches Women's Leadership Conference and the Circle of Concerned African Women Theologians. The former and its most recent version, the Millennium Women's Jubilee Conference, group churchwomen of all denominations around the challenge of a really Christian approach to the yearnings of African women. The Circle, which is multireligious, has concerned itself in the past ten years with producing relevant theology in Africa, and the Christian members have focused on issues of gospel and culture as well as the participation of women in the church.

All these Christian women have been concerned with women's leadership in the church, and all of them, whatever their religion, have faced the feminization of poverty in all its complexity and have challenged their faith communities to a positive response. They have all been concerned with the militarization and poor governance that drains Africa of its resources, and the Christian women ask: Does the church care? What women's groups talk about, what they act on, all point to the fact that society's cultural construction of gender, which the church by and large validates and promotes, is problematic for women. It seems to me therefore that to relate gospel to women is to deal with the gender construct that virtually diminishes the humanity of women and puts a stamp of approval on male entitlements.

The question then is pertinent: What does the gospel, when preached, really do to effect betterment in women's lives? Again we do not need to rehearse the experiences of women that the United Nations has been instrumental in revealing. All that is being asked of nations is that they act to end discrimination and violence against women in particular and generally for the elimination of the gender bias that favors men and discriminates against women. If the churches lived the gospel, no one would need to say this to them. The reality, however, is that the decade revealed that the church's solidarity with women falls far short of that envisaged in the gospel. Moreover, popular theology and studies keep coming up with the conclusion that Genesis 2:20-24, and 3:16 are biblical "injunctions," charges from God that explain the status of women and make what should be what is. Nothing else in biblical revelation seems to matter. This is all the more reason why we should ask the question, What is the good news of Jesus Christ in relation to women? and require the church to be accountable to God for the lives women in Africa have to live.

The reality of African Christianity today is that its popular theologians are the charismatic preachers of mass rallies, mass media, mega-churches, songwriters, gospel singers and those who generate the choruses that enliven African churches today. The words we sing appear as slogans on our vehicles and storefronts. None of this specifically deals with the challenges that women have to face, beyond counseling resignation and deliverance from Satan. What is the good news to a woman accused of being a witch because she would not submit to patriarchy but the institutionalizing agent of the might of men that seeks to control and appropriate the sexuality and reproductive services of women? In Ghana this has become institutionalized in a witches' refuge situated in Gambaga in northern Ghana. Such women face molestation and even death if they dare to return to their homes. The gospel needs to speak to this mind-set, which warps all our systems and structures. The gospel for women needs to teach and practice the biblical affirmation that all human beings are made in the image of God and are therefore worthy of honor and *shalom.*

What is the gospel to women whose call to ordained ministry is blocked by their church's adherence to Pauline injunctions? The phobia around women's expression of Christian theology has reached such proportions that it muffles people's hearing and glazes their eyes, so that when women speak in the name of Sophia, Wisdom, people do not see Wisdom at creation, Wisdom that is related to the Word, but they see the ancient Greek goddess. What is the gospel to women, whose theological reflections are ignored, dismissed, or denounced, as if only men can respond to the call and intimations from God? Wisdom demands that we understand the world we live in, and it is peopled by women and men. It stands to reason that the church's stance of requiring women to leave the thinking to men cannot be of the will of God.

What is the gospel to women, whose concern is for a spirituality that directs Christians to act responsively with regard to the quality of life of all humanity, including women? The current focus on violence against women and children is evidence of this question. The quality of one's life is measured not by the materialistic tape but by the degree of self-worth that empowers one to enjoy the gift of life. God's mission through the church ought to be an avenue for the development and enhancement of this aspect of women's lives. The widespread attitude that men come first has been captured by one researcher who observes that, "the church prefers not to violate the sanctity of the male ego!"[7] This primitive preference continues in domestic regulations that are enforced by the church that claim to be based on Paul's words, not practices, and which in Africa empower cultures to keep women in the status of minors. The good news that says not one little bird falls but God marks the event should be employed to lift women out of the so-called curse that now enables men to use the church to keep women hovering between being the image of God and being the gateway to hell. Do we really believe that with the Christ-event the sting of the curse of the fall has been removed, and that we are expected to live the original blessings bestowed at creation? With the Christ-event God should be able to look at the relationship of women and men and say, "This is good and beautiful." If the church has a Christ-centered mission this would be one of the results.

A Christ-Centered Mission

A Christ-centered mission should demonstrate its understanding of who the Christ is. Taking the word at the linguistic level, one can say that the Bible—and indeed the world—knows many who are anointed to move the human race forward in matters of morality, ethics, and spirituality. There are many who have delivered individuals and communities from bondage to other powers. We have had, do have, and I believe need to continue to have many such saviors. Given our context as Christians, the Christ we refer to is Jesus of Nazareth, whose birth, life, death, and resurrection earned him the title "the Christ." This is the two-thousand-year-old legacy of the religion that bears that name. Thus, although we discern God at work in the world and through other religions, we claim a unique involvement in God's mission through Jesus of Nazareth, designated Son of God and Anointed of God.

What then is the profile of a mission that has Jesus Christ at its center? Why was Jesus sent to earth? African women will recall immediately, "I have come that they might have life and have it

---

[7] Valentia Quame, "Christian Religions and Their Approach towards the Concerns of Women" (dissertation, University of Ghana, Legon, 1999).

in all abundance" (John 10:10). What will this mean in Africa? Since the liberal 1960s and through the vehicle of liberating theology, Luke 4:18 has been named the manifesto of Nazareth and, together with the Magnificat, has been the flag-bearer for what a Christ-centered mission should look like.

Fullness of life is incompatible with the bad news of death and exploitation that fills our world and is reflected in our media. It is incompatible with the various levels of imprisonment that we suffer. It is incompatible with our lack of physical sight and insight into what makes for our good. It is incompatible with the brokenness of the environment, body and spirit, and the victimization of "the other." Fullness of life has to do with the experience of God's favor in our individual and communal lives.

African women continue in faith and hope to sing the Magnificat, which is attributed to Mary the mother of Jesus. The Christ-centered mission should work to make it a reality that the hungry will be filled with things and the satiated rich will of course feel the emptiness of their situation. If democracy would lift the lowly and bring down the mighty it might be seen as a Christ-centered mission, and it should begin in the church, where hierarchical thinking and living operate on principles that are contrary to what Jesus says about being great and being "in power."

A Christ-centered mission should have a message that is understood. Jesus preached in stories, historical events, and contemporary experiences that were understood by his audience. The proclamation was about the reign of God, and his deeds were a demonstration that indeed God reigns. Mission centered on Christ Jesus must be in an idiom that is understood by the target audience and must touch their lives and help them make meaning of life. The proclamation must be liberative, for people need to hear "your sins are forgiven," "I will, be whole," "go and sin no more," "unbind him," "give her something to eat," "take up your mat and walk," "let the children come." If our mission is Christ-centered we shall preach Christ as God-sent and not advertise ourselves.

Much of what I read and much that I hear is about church-centered mission. The so-called Great Commission has acquired an additional phrase "organize them into churches." Church building may be inescapable, but it cannot be allowed to become the focal image and meaning of mission. If the church does what Christ did and lives the way of Christ, it can still be said to be in a Christ-centered mission. If it points a person to Jesus, whom God anointed to demonstrate to us that it is possible to live as persons made in God's image, it is surely doing mission in Christ's way.

As the second millennium of the Christian era drew to a close, a renewed interest in the ancient *Christus Victor* Christology emerged in Africa. This resurgence is the youthful expression of a vigorous faith tuned to cope with the socioeconomic challenges of Africa. It is these challenges that have fueled ethnic and religious conflicts, which have urged nations to seek political stability through militarism. The persons who feel called to this mission are usually themselves youthful men, and the women leaders are usually spouses of the men. Their mission is good news to women suffering under marital disharmony, persons seeking means of living or striving to secure them, persons with health problems and those seeking visas and diplomas. Traditionally, religion in Africa derives its validity and potency from its ability to solve life's problems. This view has been brought to bear on Christianity.[8] A Christ-centered mission must be seen to be a vehicle of abundant life and an instrument against the powers of deprivation and death.

The new apostles of the new churches in Africa have taken their mandate directly from the Gospels, and on Ghana's television you can hear them cry, "What Jesus says is what I say" and "what Jesus does, I do." They have appropriated the words of Jesus to the disciples and have made them operative. Luke 9:1 says clearly, "He now called the twelve together and gave them power and authority to overcome all the devils and to cure diseases, and sent them to proclaim the kingdom of God and to heal." This healing ministry has become a cardinal challenge for participation in the *missio Dei.*

The new missionaries have numerous disciples; indeed all whom they touch learn biblical passages to help them cope with eventualities. They teach them to others. They see healing as the central factor of the ministry of Jesus. Jesus healed physical, mental, and spiritual disabilities. Jesus healed broken lives, and the apostles in the Greek Bible did the same. Like the ministry of

---

[8] J. N. Tetteh, "The Dynamics of Prayer Camps and the Management of Women's Problems: A Core Study of Three Camps in the Eastern Region of Ghana. June 1999" (dissertation, University of Ghana, Legon, 1999).

Jesus, this ministry is all-inclusive. As J. N. Tetteh has demonstrated, however, more women than men avail themselves of the services. They attend the prayer camps to pray not only for themselves but for spouses and offspring. Like the disciples sent out two by two, these "youthful" persons in mission deliver people from the hands of demons and witches and Satan and preach prosperity to a people suffering under the burden of poverty. They instill confidence in persons, empowering them to rid themselves of fear, self-pity, and guilt. They provide them with prayers that become a spiritual protection against "the wiles of the enemy." Their mission is an invitation of Jesus to join the disciples. Is this Christ-centered? I would say it is, if by that God is glorified and thanks are returned in Jesus' name. If the Jesus-suffused context described at the beginning is anything to go by, one would say yes, this is Christ-centered mission. But there is an aspect of this buoyant youthful mission and ministry that calls for caution. The name of Satan is being magnified, and there is much fascination with the powers of demons. Those who call God by other names are being vilified, and other faith communities are being antagonized. The profile of a Christ-centered mission should invite an openness to dialogue with the other.

We are but earthen vessels, carrying a precious mission. A Christ-centered mission will point to Jesus of Nazareth and will honor the humanity of others if they stretch their hands toward God and strive to hear and do the will of God. If our lives and work are Christ-centered, we will take seriously the presence and mission of God in other faith communities. Second, we will honor the humanity of women as Christ did. There is no example in the life of Christ that puts women down or suggests that they are incapable of being full participants in God's mission or that they should be barred from leadership.

In Africa, Christian participation in the *missio Dei* will become more credible if we learn to honor the humanity of the "other" as Jesus did. If we identify and dismantle death-dealing structures that strangle Africa, we will make God's good news visible. And what would be easier than beginning by loving our neighbor— the woman/man, the person of another faith—as much as we love ourselves? Christ, women, and Muslims have become for me the key to opening a new chapter of the churches' participation in God's mission in Africa.

Response to Mercy Amba Oduyoye

Sung-Hae Kim, S.C.

WHEN I FINISHED READING MERCY AMBA ODUYOYE'S "THREE Cardinal Issues of Mission in Africa," I recalled E. E. Evans-Pritchard's book *Nuer Religion*. Even though I am not sure how well this book represents the religious life of the Nuer people and the peoples of Africa, the book imprinted in me a kind of deep respect for the African traditional religions and cultures as a whole. Evans-Pritchard showed that the concept of the Spirit (*kwoth*) who resides in heaven as the creator of everything is pure inasmuch as the Spirit is not identified with any natural phenomena but is above them all, while causing them to happen. Below the High God are many spirits who influence the concrete realities of daily life. What interested me was the fact that the relationship between the High God and the other lower spirits is sometimes very clear, but in some cases ambivalent, for it concerns the realm of mystery. Evans-Pritchard noted that the African understanding of the spiritual world reflects the social structure of the tribe, but at the same time transcends it. Their penetrating awareness of spiritual matters is most vividly exhibited by their understanding of religious rites. What is most important is sincerity of the heart, and so expensive animal sacrifices can be replaced by, for example, a cucumber, as long as the one offering the sacrifice has a pure intention. Evans-Pritchard commented that the Islamic influence was increasing for the Nuer people, but the basic worldview and belief system remains traditional.

Mercy Oduyoye chose three issues—the dialogue with Islam, the inculturation of Christian theology, and the church's role for women in Africa—as most urgent and crucial for the mission of African Christianity. At the first glance I was amazed by the fact that even though the details are different, the major issues which she chose for Africa are quite similar in East Asia as well. I will try to respond to her talk from my limited horizon and ask a few questions in order to attain a clearer vision of Africa, about which I have the least direct experience.

First, in the area of the interreligious dialogue, Oduyoye mentions the Christian churches' relationship with Islam and African religion. She sees the problems involved as different in the two cases. With Islam it is the hidden fear and mutual antipathy accumulated through a long history. She points to the dialogue movements and the work of the journal *ProCMuRA*. Having been introduced to this dialogue, we need more information on the dialogue. For example, how widespread is the dialogue with Islam and who is involved in it? Are African bishops, priests, ministers, and religious, as well as theologians actively participating? More importantly, are leaders of the churches offering education for interreligious dialogue for future generations through seminary training, seminars, books, and personal encounters?

Oduyoye points out that the general attitude of Christians and Muslims toward the adherents of African religion is characterized by pride or superiority. I was amused reading it, for in South Korea we have the same problem. Korean Christians and Buddhists, who comprise half of the population, also feel contempt toward Shamanistic practices, new religions, and even toward traditional cultures such as Confucianism and Taoism. More Christians are willing to learn from the Buddhist meditation and philosophy of emptiness (although even here some Christian leaders hold hidden fear and antagonism), but the folk belief based on the Shaman's rituals is condemned as superstition. It took us three decades of scholarly research to explore the deep religiosity of Korean Shamanism and additional personal encounters with the Shamans in order to begin a kind of table conversation. But because of the lack of scholarly training on the part of the Shamans, Christian dialogue with Shamanism still depends largely on the anthropologists who have field experience. Christian dialogue with Confucian scholars and Taoist researchers again has a different color and tone, since it focuses more on the formation of personal and communal utopia. In a word, Korean Christians look for different themes when we begin the dialogue. In conversation with Buddhists, meditation methods and cultural adaption are explored; with the Confucians, the focus is on personal growth and social ethics; with Taoists it centers on artistic creativity in relation with nature; and with Shamans, it examines healing rituals, blessing, and life after death. One of the key issues Oduyoye raises is certainly the need radically to rethink African traditional religiosity and to gain insight into how Christians can overcome their "illusory" sense of superiority over the adherents of African traditional religion.

Second, Oduyoye notes that many problems flow from a church-centered concept of mission, and she advocates a return to a Christ-centered mission. A church-centered mission, as I understand it, is the Christian misunderstanding which appropriates *Christus Victor* Christology into a church-building business. According to her, recently there is a renewed resurgence of this tendency in the youthful African churches, which fuels ethnic and religious conflicts. There are analogies to this need in our relations with fast-growing "new" churches in South Korea. A competitive spirit still persists in the fundamentalist-oriented conservative Protestant churches. But recently the growth rate of the Christian converts has drastically decreased, and the need of dialogue is felt more vividly. Oduyoye is certainly correct in saying that there is a constant temptation for the Christian mission to be overly church-centered and concerned with institutional success. Christians in mission and in all their communities must listen to the voice of the prophets to be purified from this self-seeking tendency.

Then what is the Christ-centered mission that Oduyoye advocates? She is looking for the ideal profile of a mission that has Jesus Christ at its center: "A Christ-centered mission will point to Jesus of Nazareth and will honor the humanity of others." After quoting John 10:10 she asks, "What will this mean in Africa?" The Christian proclamation must be liberative for sinners, the broken environment, and the victimized. In her appeal for a Christ-centered mission I hear a call to return to the original gospel of Jesus, but at the same time I am not completely satisfied with this, for I can hear the same answer from many other parts of the world in this century. I would like to hear a particular answer that can come only from Africa or from a part of Africa at the dawn of the twenty-first century. Not only do we have to accept the gospel of Jesus, which is clothed in ancient Jewish language, but we also have to interpret it with our cultural language in order to give a richer and more vivid meaning to it. How will the Christ-centered mission be incarnated in Africa? What will be the answer of African Christian churches to the worldwide ecological crisis? What I am trying to say is that not only does the Christian gospel challenge our traditional culture, but also the original insights of our cultural traditions, which were undoubtedly inspired by the Holy Spirit, have to transform the color of Christian questions and probe the hidden dimensions of the Christian gospel. So I want to hear what the African concept of Christian mission will be both in theory and in practice.

Third, Oduyoye notes that the church in Africa empowers cultures to keep women in the status of minors by preferring not to violate the sanctity of the male ego. I found it very interesting because her comment is almost the same as the comment of a Korean Catholic anthropologist, Cho Okla, who said that the prejudice against women is even stronger in the church than in the world. It is commonly pointed out in South Korea that the Catholic Church's centralized authority structure with male priesthood has reinforced the patriarchal Confucian discrimination against women, in spite of the fact that women comprise the majority of the faithful. I hope to see the day when men and women enjoy true equality in every aspect of church life, not only spiritual and salvational, but cultural and institutional as well. But at the same time I treasure and want to work out the salvation of women and men through Jesus' teaching and the insights of Confucius, Lao Tzu, and the sages of different cultures. I am sure that if I learn more of African religious songs and wisdom sayings, I will learn some aspect of God that I do not know now. Therefore, even in the area of the liberation of women in its full sense, I would like draw out from the age-old treasures and give a new contemporary color. In this sense, I would like to ask Oduyoye to illustrate a little more what kind of African materials she thinks can be useful to restore women to their original state of dignity?

4

Evangelization of Europe?

Observations on a Church in Peril

Peter Hünermann

The Problem

EVANGELIZATION AND MISSION IN EUROPE ARE BEING increasingly discussed, as the old distinction between sending and receiving churches in mission loses all geographical orientation. Yet the question is much more complex than the *instrumentum laboris* of the Special Synod of European Bishops suggests.[1] An answer to this question presupposes a self-critique of the European church and a readiness for repentance and conversion that I fail to see in the call of the pope to evangelize Europe, and also in the pronouncements of the Roman Curia in the last two decades. One cannot overcome a crisis of this proportion in the European church by putting it under taboo, glossing over the facts, and covering it up.

We begin our reflections regarding the church as an institution within European society. I summarize the facts to be considered in a series of theses. Each will be stated in a straightforward manner. I will then briefly discuss the evidence for the thesis as stated.

---

[1] Bischofssynode, Zweite Sonderversamlung für Europa, *Jesus Christus, der lebt in seiner Kirche: Quellen der Hoffnung für Europa, Instrumentum laboris* (Bonn: Sekretariat der Deutschen Bischofskonferenz, 1999).

This has the advantage of stating issues boldly, and the disadvantage of making it appear that the complexity of the issue is dealt with adequately in the simple statement. I realize fully how multifaceted the questions dealt with are.

Thesis 1
The European church as institution is in a process of dissolution.

By "institution" I mean the church as a public and normative form of interaction and communication that makes possible a certain orientation in life and society, enabling people to relate to one another. Every communication, every interaction, every relationship to the facts of the matter involved in the call for a "reevangelization" of Europe presupposes institutions. If my thesis is correct—that the Catholic Church in Europe is involved in a dramatic process of dissolution—the central and focal point and mission of Christian life are in peril. In short, then, I am saying that Christian life lived publicly by the church's members in and according to the gospel as an engagement with the message of Jesus Christ and the translation of that into daily life is dwindling and even becoming impossible.

Let me cite a series of facts to corroborate my thesis. People in ministry are an essential part of the church; they render services to people so that individuals, groups, and communities may live a life of faith. In considering the data, I was astonished to see that the developments in France, Germany, and other Western European countries (albeit with some differences in stages in the various countries) are all going in the same direction. Let me begin with the French statistics.[2] Between 1900 and 1950 the number of ordinations of diocesan clergy dropped about 33 percent. From 1950, this process of decline accelerated considerably. From 1000 ordinations per year in 1950, the number dropped continuously to 500 by the beginning of the 1970s. At the beginning of the 1980s there were about 175 ordinations per year. At the beginning of the 1990s, 110 ordinations were recorded. From then on the number has been around 100 per year. The average age of the clergy in France in the mid-1990s was around sixty-

---

[2] For the following, see Bernard Sesboüé, *N'ayez pas peur! Regards sur l'Eglise et les ministères aujourd'hui* (Paris, 1999).

five. Only 5 percent of the total number of French priests were younger than forty. Fifty-six of the 96 French dioceses had fewer than one ordination per year between 1974 and 1991. Thirty-six averaged one to two ordinations per year; only two dioceses averaged four to six. One diocese in the same period had four to five ordinations, and in Paris ordinations came to five to six per year.

Regarding religious, one finds a very similar development. In 1950, about 680 entered male congregations and orders. By 1991, the number had dropped to 150. On the average there were 50 professions of religious per year in the period from 1975 to 1991. The number of women in congregations and orders dwindled at about the same rate. From the end of the 1960s to 1995, the apostolic or active congregations and orders of women lost about 50 percent of their membership. At the same time, the average age rose to above sixty-five, and today about 5 percent of the sisters are under the age of fifty.

The corresponding numbers for Germany are equally alarming. In 1952 Bishop Keller of Münster wrote in a pastoral letter that the shortage of priests was his greatest concern.[3] A year later he spoke on the decline in the number of sisters.[4] He foresaw a critical point in the beginning of the 1980s for the various institutions of the diocese staffed by sisters. In fact this point was reached *at the end of the 1960s.* At the beginning of the 1970s, the number of diocesan and religious priests in Germany was 26,206. In 1997 there were 11, 000 diocesan priests and 2,000 religious.[5] That means a decrease of 50 percent in twenty-five years. By 2010 there will have been another decline of 50 percent of active diocesan and religious priests, due to the disproportionate number of elderly priests.

The statistics in Italy, Spain, the Netherlands, and Belgium are very similar. What are the effects? H. Simon writes regarding France:

It began with a diminution of the numbers of priests and religious or sisters teaching in schools, especially Catholic secondary schools . . . then the increasing scarcity of priests

---

[3] See Wilhelm Damberg, *Abschied vom Milieu? Katholizismus im Bistum Münster und in den Niederlanden 1945-1980* (Paderborn, 1997), 186-87.

[4] See Gerhard Schmittchen, *Priester in Deutschland* (Freiburg, 1973).

[5] *Berufung: Zur Pastoral der geistlichen Berufe,* no. 37 (1999): 38-39.

in pastoral centers for school children, and then the disappearance of associate pastors in rural areas. Parallel to this has been a meltdown of the number of sisters working in nursing and catechesis. Finally, we are witnessing the erosion of priest-teams. Where we had three, two remained, then one. Today we move towards zero in many cases.[6]

The thinning out of ecclesiastical institutions by drastic reductions in the numbers of priests and religious is only one indication of a wider process that produces a series of effects. It puts younger priests at special risk. They are stationed much more often on their own and are often overburdened with too many responsibilities. The deterioration of the ecclesiastical milieu makes personal and spiritual maturation much more difficult. In the light of all this, the criteria for selection of candidates are often unrealistic, and the pastoral situation, with the innumerable frustrations that young priests experience, would require extraordinarily mature persons. Ordinary men, faced with such difficulties, fall into a difficult situation of isolation. Moreover, a growing number of them come from traditionalist circles and milieus. They are characterized by traditionalist liturgical preferences and a very strongly authoritarian pastoral style. Some of them cling very much to external signs and practices, such as wearing the Roman collar. All these are often symptoms of a high level of fragility.

Corresponding to these data about church ministry are data about the situation of the People of God in Europe. We summarize these facts in the following thesis.

Thesis 2
According to the statistical data about baptisms, weddings, Sunday mass attendance, and the Christian socialization of children and teenagers, the People of God in Europe since 1950 has shrunk and continues to shrink at an ever-growing rate.

The statistics are extraordinary. Among the many I could choose, please consider the following as a sample. According to

---

[6] H. Simon, *Documents-épiscopat*, no. 8 (April 1992): 2.

1987 data, fewer than 60 percent of the children in France are baptized, and fewer than 40 percent of all children receive catechetical instruction. The number of church marriages has fallen below 50 percent. Attendance at weekly Sunday mass is between 5 and 10 percent. A vast majority of the Europeans do not profess the essentials of the Christian creed. This is regarding belief in a personal God, the divinity of Christ, not to mention death and eternal life.[7]

What does this mean? Minimally, the data represent a slide into a loss of fundamental conviction about the truth of Christian faith. In addition, there is a tremendous loss of "Christian memory" in Europe. In many families one cannot speak of a transmission of the faith from parents to children. A considerable proportion of younger parents are unable to answer questions their children ask about religious matters and problems.

This leads to my third thesis.

Thesis 3
The religious climate of European society is characterized by a pluralism of religions, on the one hand, and large blocks of the population who are without any religion, on the other.

Let us take France as an example for the traditional Catholic countries. France has a population of 57 million people with about 45 million baptized Catholics. Thus, Catholics represent nearly 80 percent of the population. The next group is made up of slightly over 4 million Muslims. Their number is continuously increasing because of their high birth rate and immigration, especially from northern Africa. Protestants and Orthodox form a group of 1.1 million. There are also about 650,000 Jews and about 600,000 Buddhists. This leaves a group of about 5 million (10 percent) who are listed as not being members of any public confession. But in surveys, 47 percent of the French population consider themselves as areligious or atheistic! This can only mean that many who are carried on Catholic Church membership rolls should not be on them.

---

[7] See Paul Zulehner and Hermann Denz, *Wie Europa lebt und glaubt: Europäische Wertstudie* (Düsseldorf, 1993), 17-55.

Germany is a country that has for generations had a roughly equal mixture of Catholics and Protestants, and we observe the same trends there as in France. One-third of the population is listed officially as Catholic and one-third as Protestant. There is a considerable group of people without any religion: they constitute 70 percent of the population of the former East Germany, and slightly more than 10 percent in the West. But in surveys 38 percent of the people from West Germany consider themselves areligious or atheistic. There is a strong Muslim population, especially in big cities such as Berlin, Stuttgart, Frankfurt, Duisburg, and the like, where Muslim children represent 20 to 30 percent of the school-age children. The total number of Muslims is 3.3 million.

More important than numbers are the religious climate and the opinions that result from the everyday experience of religious pluralism. In the large "Europe Value Studies," a very small percentage of young people believe that there is one true religion. The vast majority are convinced that there are truths to be found in each of the great world religions. Claims of absoluteness of religion are utterly repudiated as a kind of fundamentalism or integralism. The conflict in Northern Ireland, controversies between Orthodox and Muslims in the former Yugoslavia and Islamic fundamentalism are seen as perverse attitudes.

The Catholic Church is seen in this context as one religious community among others. The word of the church gains credibility only insofar as the life of its communities in a given country gives a vivid testimony of faith. The notion or even the possibility of infallible magisterium teaching that the Catholic Church is given a special position in the plan of God is viewed as incomprehensible and improbable, especially among young people. Making such claims provokes general disapproval.

Thus far, I have referred mainly to Western Europe, especially to France and Germany. The situation in the Central European countries such as the Czech Republic, Slovakia, Hungary, Croatia, Latvia, Lithuania, Estonia, Rumania, and Poland has been dramatically affected by their history in the post–World War II era. Thus there are peculiarities proper to these countries, but there are also many similarities between Central and Western Europe. With the exception of Poland, there are, in all these countries, significant groups of the population who adhere to no religious tradition. Of course there are differences in the various nations. Czechs, Latvians, and Hungarians include a higher proportion of areligious people than one finds among the Slovaks. The lowest percentage of nonaffiliation is in Poland. As a matter of fact, the contemporary culture of Central Europe is largely shaped by *areligious* people. In all these countries, with the exception of Poland, ecclesiastical institutions are weak and fragile. They have had to be restored with great difficulty after the collapse of the Soviet empire. Vocations have not been numerous. The special difficulty in Poland was—and is—that the church as institution was strictly anti-Communist. The new situation of being a church in a modern, pluralistic, democratic society has proven difficult for a leadership accustomed to being in opposition and now wanting to return to an era when they had greater influence. It is commonly observed that Poles, upon emigrating to Western countries, often alter their religious attitudes. Many of them, in fact, give up their Catholic practice within a short period of time.

In this general situation, the European episcopacy has a twofold option. On the one hand, there is a more or less traditionalist option, with a strong emphasis on restoration. Following that option, every innovation is suspected of being an accommodation to secularism. It seems to me that this restorationist goal is currently dominant in the Roman Curia. It has a history that dates back to the Second Vatican Council. As a symbol of that attitude's strength, consider the fact that Pope Paul VI, in the address given to the members of the commission for the reform of Canon Law, did not quote any of the documents of Vatican II. He referred only to Pius XII and his vision of law in the church. And it is precisely this new code that is appealed to in most practical decisions, truncating contested experiments, innovations, or changes.

To be sure, in the various bishops' conferences the traditionalist bishops are a minority. But they are a very effective minority, because of the support they receive from the Roman Curia. One thinks of the endless quarrels in the Dutch Bishops' Conference, the eleven years of Bishop Haas in Chur and his subsequent appointment as archbishop in Liechtenstein, the painful affair of

Cardinal Groer in Vienna, the chronicle of Bishop Krenn in St. Pölten. To these affairs can be added issues such as the problem of the counseling service for pregnant women in Germany or the case of the oath of fidelity, in which the German Bishops' Conference was silent for ten years, attempting to avoid implementing this directive. The Congregation of the Doctrine of the Faith recently insisted that they implement the oath, something that has had disastrous consequences for the credibility of clergy and theologians. A majority in the bishops' conferences may see things in a more nuanced and modern than restorationist manner, but they find themselves under enormous pressure to conform to the wishes of the Curia.

The polarization of bishops finds its equivalent in the split between traditionalist Christians, on the one hand, and the vast majority of Christians, on the other. Generally speaking, European traditionalist Christians are very well organized and enjoy broad access to the mass media.[8] On the other side, the movement "We Are the Church" collected over one million signatures in Germany alone, most from regular Sunday mass attendees. They made a loud appeal, but in the end, one gets the impression that their appeal went unheard.

The picture that I have sketched here of the European church as institution is incomplete. Parallel to the silent earthquake destroying the traditional house of faith something new is blooming. The enormous losses and collapses are not being balanced off by these first signs of a potentially different future. But it is important to note what is new and qualitatively different. It is not simply a restoration. To understand what these new sprouts portend for the destiny of the church in Europe, we must ask: What are the reasons for the silent earthquake? How is it happening? What perspectives might be gained from insights into the reasons for its occurrence?

---

[8] For a good overview of the traditionalist groups in Germany, see Klaus Nientiedt, "Gefürchtet, überschätzt, dämonisiert: Rechtskonservative Gruppierungen im deutschen Katholizismus," *Herder Korrespondenz* 49 (1995): 487-92.

Reasons for the Current Crisis

We begin this new series of questions by summarizing our reflections in thesis form:

Thesis 4
The current crisis of the European church is linked to the crisis of the transformation of European society in modernity, in which the basic characteristics of the emerging society are in discontinuity with the institutional structure of the church.

This thesis presupposes that the community of the faithful, in confessing the one faith, *must develop institutional features linked to the form and characteristics of public life in the age in which it finds itself.* The necessity of doing this becomes obvious if one takes into account that the *Catholic* tradition's orientation to the Christian faith involves affirming a certain link between faith and the rational truths commonly and publicly affirmed in a given epoch. Catholicism has refused the sectarian option of withdrawing into a holy community separate from the world. Instead, it has virtually always and everywhere taken shape in a way consonant with the idea that God can only be confessed in faith as creator and redeemer of humankind and of history to the extent that connections and linkages are made between rational truths and fundamental insights into secular realities, on the one hand, and the articles of faith, on the other. This involves the necessity of *inculturating* faith. It is obvious that the social structures of the community of the faithful are shaped accordingly. This is not simply an accommodation to the spirit of the times; the structures proper to the church must be compatible with the fundamental principles of social life, and around this accommodation there is always debate and dialogue. As we examine this issue in more detail, the need for these abstract reflections will become clearer and our intention will be clarified as well.

How should we describe the essential lines of the transformation of European society in modernity? There are innumerable books, as well as sociological, political, and cultural analyses available that seek to understand this process. In order to come to terms with the massive amount of literature available so as to arrive at common ground, we begin with the self-understanding of modern men and women in Europe. I am articulating here not a sophisticated philosophical thesis but a fundamental matter-of-fact attitude that crystallizes around the self-understanding of Europeans concerning concrete human rights. Human rights are discussed and demanded everywhere, even if they are often violated and recognized in their absence. Declarations of human rights and respect for them are decisive criteria for nations seeking entry into the European Union (EU). Although many would make it seem that the most important thing for the EU is transparent reporting of economic data, constraining inflation, reducing public debt, this is not how Europeans see the matter. Rather, respect for human rights is seen as the *sine qua non* for the EU to grow.

What are the institutional conditions for the possibility of guaranteeing human rights? Generally speaking, it is recognized that human rights do not have a chance if there is not a strict differentiation of legislative, executive, and judicial institutions in a given society. If the executive branch dominates the courts, the guarantee of human rights will be empty. The distinctive nature and independence of the judiciary from the executive imply a legislative dimension that recognizes the inviolability of human rights and can coerce the executive to secure such rights. Such functional differentiation of public power is an essential aspect of modern European society. On this point different political and sociological schools of thought are of a single mind. This kind of separation of powers is absolutely necessary.

In addition, there must be a corresponding framework of public opinion and a public sphere in which to bring public opinion to bear. The modern rule of law and the constitutional state, from their very beginnings, have prospered as they gave public access to court proceedings. At the same time the legislative branch had to secure the power to monitor and to compel a flow of information from an executive branch that was often loath to grant it. This change of understanding of the flow of information and checks and balances, in their turn, became possible only because of the pressure exercised by print media free to operate in the public sphere.

This realm of freedom of speech in a public sphere has come to be seen as unconditionally necessary with regard not only to fundamental human rights but also to various rights closely connected to them, such as freedom of opinion, freedom of association, freedom for scientific research, the freedom of the press, and so forth. All these rights presuppose public media that purvey the full variety of opinions that exist in a free society. Recognition of this approach to human rights, in turn, implies the possibility of constituting public forums, even if those in power do not like them or approve the opinions expressed in them.

I draw two conclusions about modern European society from these brief reflections. Modern European society is characterized by functional differentiation of power, and not just in the realm of national, state, or supranational political order. Modern society is functionally differentiated as a whole. The economic system, the educational system, the defense system, the health system, and so forth affect society as a whole, albeit in different and specific ways. Economic life, for instance, conditions the whole of a given society, albeit in a specific way. The educational system affects the entire society, and yet must be distinguished from the economic sphere in a specific way. Each sphere has a relative independence while being part of an interdependent whole. Moreover, all societal activities structure themselves with relative freedom in the public sphere. One cannot imagine economy without marketing and advertising. The army, the universities, and schools need public relations efforts. The health system cannot do without the communication media. Insurance companies and pension funds must "go public" to spread risk if they want to avoid serious damage in the case of a large-scale disaster.

All these social agents, each enjoying its specific form in the public sphere, are also in competition with one another for resources and power. Public attention and awareness are important measures of influence and power. It is only through attention and awareness, mediated through the construction of the public sphere, that a society can attain the efficacy it needs to thrive.

The different features of the public sphere, generated by the various social agents, are marked by specific interests. In this they reveal their specific limits as well. Reflecting their special interests, they also convey an image or ideal of what it means to be a man or a woman, a vision of successful life and satisfying social relationships, a vision of the world and how to live in that world. To some extent, these visions compete with one another in contemporary society.

Such modern societies are information societies. This does not mean that information is merely one characteristic of society among others. Rather, the development, possession, and dissemination of information are foundational characteristics of society. Modern Europeans live in a plurality of structures of the public sphere, and individuals live with the possibility of creating their roles and patterns of behavior as they choose. These characteristics of modern society are profoundly at variance with the social structure that the Catholic Church is trying today to maintain, and this is a large part of the problem of the church in Europe today. This leads us to our fifth thesis.

Thesis 5
The institutional structure of the church is still deeply imbued with and operating from a concept of society that most Europeans consider obsolete.

The contrast between the features of modern European society and the social and institutional structures of the church become clear when one considers the traditional vision of European society. These characteristics can be summarized in three principles:

- The *polis* as a whole prevails over the individual. Aristotle argued in favor of that principle, emphasizing that the human individual can develop his human potential only through the *polis*. This is considered a law of nature. From this idea Aristotle deduces the qualities of the ruler and the rights of those who have those qualities to be the rulers.

- Only the ruler (or the ruling group) may represent or speak for the whole *polis*. Only in the ruler can the whole *polis* be seen. Indeed, the empire or the *polis* is constituted by the headship of ruler.

- Only the ruler can discern the interests of the *polis* as a whole, since individuals and groups follow their particular interests and cannot see the needs of the whole.

I call this the traditional vision of European society. The three principles are to be considered pragmatic leitmotifs. To be sure, political theories are always much more complex and differentiated. Aristotle speaks of various types of organization of the polis. Thomas Aquinas explores how to avoid tyranny. But politics and social life are zones not primarily of theoretical knowledge but of practical choice making. Throughout European history, from the days of the Roman empire through the era of "enlightened absolutism" in the eighteenth century, public order exemplified this vision and its dynamic. The history of modern Europe began in the ongoing struggle to contain its extremes.

It is obvious that this traditional vision or concept of European society is opposed to the vision of a modern European society. The modern European protests strenuously if one tries to coerce the individual to follow the dictates of the whole, because in such submission modernity sees inviolable human dignity endangered and human rights disrespected. I hasten to concede that the "whole" and the "common good" *are* important and cannot be neglected. But the whole and the common good are limited as to what they can demand under the contemporary view of respect for human rights. Indeed, it is probably not too much to say that it is presumed today that only when individual human rights are respected is the value of the common good guaranteed.

Referring to the second principle enunciated above, it is evident to the modern European that the constitution, which is an expression of how the whole relates to the parts, is the basis of the state's legitimacy and not the authority of ruler. To govern a modern state entails performing a functionally limited service to the common weal.

The third principle of older European society is categorically rejected by modern Europeans. It is hard to imagine anyone favoring the concentration of public power in the hands of an absolute ruler. Instead, complex structures are devised so that the interests of the whole are respected and protected from the despot. The path to realizing this concept of society has been a very long and painful one. In that process, functional differentiations of roles and rights in society have been developing since the Middle Ages. Important milestones were the distinction between spiritual and temporal power in the Concordat of Worms in 1122, the invention of the printing press, the introduction of universal primary education, the Enlightenment, and the codification of human rights. It is evident that the church was positively involved in many aspects of this history.

Having presented some of the features of modern European society as well as those of its predecessors, we can ask: To what extent is the Catholic Church in our time still characterized by the traditional European vision?

First, in a preliminary observation, we should recognize that the first chapter of the Vatican II Dogmatic Constitution on the Church, *Lumen Gentium,* speaks of the church *as mystery.* That is to say, *Lumen Gentium* speaks of the salvific decision of God, the salvific mission of the Word made flesh, and the salvific efficacy of the Holy Spirit. In the next chapter, the church is presented as the People of God present in all times and generations. To speak of the church as an institution, as we have been above, is to examine another aspect of the church. As an institution, the church has to embody socially and historically the mysterious, divine-vocation aspect of its nature. Still, lest we want to totally bifurcate the institutional and divine-mystery aspects, the reality of being the People of God must be represented as adequately as possible in its institutional aspects. The church as institution is not fully and in all aspects identical with both the *mysterium ecclesiae* and the People of God. The church as institution has undergone a very complex history that was marked by a sharp turn toward juridical self-definition in the Middle Ages. Yves Congar called it an ecclesiological turnaround.[9] The juridical view of the church is also linked closely to the older European vision and realization of societal construction. This affected the constitution of the church as institution in countless ways. Today we stand at a place where modern techniques of social control and centralized management have merged with these two trends of the past to create a central administration with unprecedented power.

Within the Catholic Church today one finds the principle that the "universal church" as institution—meaning what the central

---

[9] Yves Congar, *Die Lehre von der Kirche: Von Augustinus bis zum abendländischen Schisma,* Handbuch der Dogmengeschichte III/3c (Freiburg/Basel/Vienna: Herder, 1971), 53-76.

administration says it means—enjoying priority over all individuals, groups, communities, and local churches of whatever size. There is no independent administrative court before which a diocese can plead its rights against the Roman Curia. There is no provision in canon law that gives the faithful a way to demand their right to receive the sacraments when church law creates structures that impede access to them. In this regard, there are many communities and parishes that have no priest. To whom can they appeal for relief? Who can judge in their favor over against the central administration of the church? Just one example. In the discussions in the German Pastoral Synod and in a number of diocesan synods, clergy and laity asked for a reform of the conditions for ordination. It went nowhere, yet there is no means to compel a public hearing of their plea. In effect, there is no essential limitation on the ruler of the church. The dignity and the legitimate interests of individuals, groups, communities, and local churches are not protected by the right of a formal appeal either to a legislative or a judicial branch. Take as another example the pastoral service of counseling for pregnant women in Germany. Granted that it was complicated by the debated question of how to handle the question of abortion. Still, the Catholic Church carried out this ministry for some twenty years. It was ended under public pressure from Rome, despite a series of near unanimous decisions from the German bishops (the only dissenting voice was Bishop Dyba, a notorious traditionalist). Roman interests and judgments prevailed purely and simply over local interests and judgments on how to handle this complex question.

The theory lurking behind this practice is the same as that which undergirded the whole of traditional European society, namely, that the pope or the bishops represent the whole church, and that the church is constituted from this point of origin. The original schema on the church for Vatican II—prepared by the theological commission chaired by Cardinal Ottaviani, with the Jesuit Sebastian Tromp serving as secretary—was formally based on this idea. Under this paradigm, Jesus had received all power and authority from his Father. This *potestas* was handed on to the apostles, and then to the bishops, especially Peter and his successors. The church, the community of the People of God, was imaged as resulting from this conferral of hierarchical authority.[10] The concept was found doubtful by the majority of the council fathers. *Lumen Gentium* placed statements about the *mysterium ecclesiae* and the People of God at the beginning of the document and only later introduced the hierarchical constitution of the church. But how difficult it proved to alter the older concept and to appropriate this new idea became evident in the fourth session of the council. The decree on the missionary activity of the church, *Ad Gentes*, had been rejected earlier, at the end of the third session. At the beginning of the fourth session a new group of theologians, moderated by Johannes Schütte, superior general of the Divine Word Missionaries, presented a new text. His collaborators in developing the new text were Yves Congar and Joseph Ratzinger, as well as Josef Neuner. Delivered in October 1965, the new text ironically advanced the old hierarchical concept of the church.[11] The beginning of the text describes the mission of the Son and the Holy Spirit as the foundation of all missionary activity of the church. Then there appears a real narrowing in the text. Peter and the apostles receive *potestas* from Christ, and the bishops are seen the heirs of the apostles. There is no reflection on the difference between the authority of Christ and the authority of the apostles, no difference between the apostles and the bishops. Regarding Pentecost, the text presupposes that the Holy Spirit came only upon the Twelve. The consequence of this is that mission is the task of the bishops, and the rest of the People of God participate in the missionary activity *of the bishops*. Cardinal Alfrink protested against this vision in the schema during the debate, referring to *Lumen Gentium*. Responding, Father Schütte conceded that it was possible to put the accent differently, but said that the commission had been inclined to accentuate the role of the bishops. In the final redaction of the text, the hierarchical feature was mitigated somewhat. Still, if one knows the history of the text and the debate—despite the sincerity of the drafters of *Ad Gentes*—one still feels the presence of this underlying hierarchical concept of the church as an institution constituted by the *potestas* of the pope and the bishops.

---

[10] *Acta Synodalia Sacrosancti Concilii Oecumenici Vaticani II* (Vatican City: Typis Polyglottis Vaticanis, 1974-78), I, IV, 12-17.

[11] Ibid., IV, III, 663-692.

That it is still widely held that only the pope, the bishops, and (in a subordinated fashion) the clergy may care for the interests of the whole can be quite clearly seen in the Roman Instruction in 1997 (cosigned by eight Congregations of the Pope's Curia), regarding the principles for the help and collaboration of lay people with ordained ministers in the carrying out of their tasks. Lay people can only give advice; they may not participate in decision making. This may be done only by the ordained.

It is not bad faith that led the church to take on the older European concept of society in the past. The church develops its social structures in interaction with the societies in which it lives, adapting itself to the concepts and assumptions present in any given society. That does not mean that the church simply reproduces these data and structures. It tries to use them according to the spirit of the gospel. But the presentation of the issue I have been developing shows that *the church has not done the same in the case of modernization in the past two hundred years as it has in the case of other periods in its history.* This difficulty of coming to terms with modernity hinders the church in fulfilling its role as sign and sacrament of God's salvific will for all peoples and nations. To give witness in a substantive way, the legitimate features of modern society must be allowed their moment in constituting the church as an institution *for the sake of the gospel.* Only by so articulating the gospel in this new way will the church be able to be the visible sign of God's grace.

There are many instances in Europe where a new type of church is appearing. A new type of Catholic, who knows theology and knows how to experience reality and make judgments on the implications of the gospel for society, is clearly in evidence. These women and men are highly motivated and have a great sense of responsibility. The number of volunteers helping out in communities and coming from their ranks has never been so great. What would happen if Catholic communities were not able to count on the innumerable women and men who prepare family and children's liturgies, coordinate youth groups, and the like? The intensive way in which people have participated in synods, roundtable discussions, diocesan pastoral councils, and so forth is an indicator of the birth of a new kind of church. The retreat movement and interest in spiritual direction also show the seriousness of these new beginnings. There are many preparing to provide this spiritual assistance to their fellow Christians. Among other things, the education of large numbers of lay theologians has contributed to this development, and no one can eliminate them from the life of the European church. Today deacons are starting to become more and more an incentive for forming a truly diaconal, serving church. That does not mean that the dein-stitutionalization of the church has stopped or been turned around. The struggle for a new form of church has been by no means decided. The vital question is whether there is anywhere a legitimation for such a new structure, a new form of the church. For the answer we must go to the texts of Vatican II.

A New Form of Church

Once again, we summarize our discussion in the form of a thesis:

Thesis 6
It must be admitted that Vatican II is marked by an ecclesiology that perpetuates the older European concept of society, but alongside this appears a new vision of the church as the community of the faithful constituted in its public form by the Word of God and the dynamism of the Holy Spirit.

The Dogmatic Constitution on Revelation, *Dei Verbum;* the Dogmatic Constitution on the Church, *Lumen Gentium;* and the Decree on the Missionary Activity of the Church, *Ad Gentes,* all begin the same way. They speak of the origin of the Word in God the Father, the procession of the Holy Spirit, and the missions of Word and Spirit in the world. From these processions they delineate the main features of the Old Testament, the Christ-event, the development of the church, the concretization of revelation in Scripture and tradition, and the mission of the church to the nations.

The point of departure is the most profound and universal divine event which opens all horizons, the horizons of creation and redemption. In this opening all truths are implied. This open space is where people may dwell in freedom, and this possibility is to be witnessed to and realized through the People of God. It is by their testimony that this divine universal open space, the divine "public sphere," is present in the world of history. All people are invited into this public sphere, but not all enter into it. It is the People of God (or perhaps more accurately followers of Christ) who are the historical subject and social agent of this open public space, and this community is constituted through the invitation of God to enter into it.

This basic concept of church in *Lumen Gentium, Dei Verbum,* and *Ad Gentes* is very similar in its structures to the main features of modern European society. We saw how the various socially different agents are always connected with the respective public sphere and their framework of publicly constituted relations. They could not exist without those relations. The church—constituted by this divine space—is similar to all these forms of social agents, but the church is also profoundly different. The church sets forth a lasting and all-encompassing horizon. It is within this horizon that the People of God as community and the sense and the meaningfulness of the People of God and of all humankind are constituted.

An Intuition of the Church in Modern European Society

Let me state the case I seek to advance in thesis form.

Thesis 7
Modern European society is characterized by a multitude of competing public spheres or frameworks of public interaction, each of which carries with it a vision and an interpretation of the human and of reality. There is competition among them regarding what will be accepted as the fundamental orientation for human beings. The structure of the church can be conceived only in a certain contrast to these social frameworks. The "public sphere" of the church does not result from worry, fear, and care for life. The church does not live from a dynamic of possessing, improving, and assuring possibilities of life. The church is constituted through God's turning toward and attending to it and an unconditioned reconciliation of its members with God. Faith can be articulated only by humans having their own identity medi-

*ated to them by opening the given public spheres beyond their
limits, humanizing in this way modern European society.*

The exclusiveness, inner logic, and limitations of the various
public spheres inevitably produce rigid and impermeable margin-
alizations. In the name of the logic of economics or the logic of
the markets, in the name of national security states or public
order, things are imposed that violate the human rights of individual men and women, groups and nations. All these particular
logics and pragmatic rules have dehumanizing consequences, if
they are not integrated, and thus relativized and limited. This is
the point where faith becomes practical. The memory of Christ
must be translated—or, more precisely, it must be realized—in a
specific way of life and action that springs from faith and trans-
forms the established social order and logic.

This new situation in which the church finds itself requires
fresh thinking. As long as the older European social concepts pre-
dominated, there was but one public sphere. It was constituted by
the respective rule or ruling group or caste. In that situation,
Christian faith had the character of a Christian culture and society. To be baptized was a social "must." The handing on of faith
to the next generation was not distinguished from the educational
process of the appropriation of one's own culture. This situation
of identity between faith and society, between faith and culture,
has vanished.

A new approach to mission, witness to the gospel, and conversion need to be given priority in the modern European church.
Fortunately, we have a slowly growing number of adult baptisms
in most of the European countries. Men and women in the adult
catechumenate are of various types. Many grew up without any
religion. There are people between twenty and thirty years of age
who were baptized but never had any real contact with Christians, and so were not able to profess their latent faith. Similar
conversions happen in youth centers. The basic fact is that people find a new identity within the process of conversion. They
begin to live in the public space God opens up for them. From
that point of identity they discover new relationships with other
people, and another view of their own situation.

Efforts to create these missionary centers in Europe are still too
weak to counterbalance the erosion of the church structures that

have long been in place. In many cases, these newly converted people do not feel at home in existing communities. All the charisms of life in the church are needed—those of married and single people, priests and religious, theologians and social workers, men and women—are needed to make contacts and carry out the work in these missionary centers for both adults and young people. We need them in every rural district and in every town.

Christians need communities to celebrate the memory of Christ's death and resurrection, to be renewed by his word, by common prayer and praise. Christians need to be reinforced in their own identity. This raises the question of the basis on which communities ought to be constituted. It is evident that our existing communities are not homogeneous, and so they try to reach people's needs by accommodating to a pastor's or a pastoral committee's ideas of a common denominator. Yet people are different because they live in very different environments, in different worlds and in different public spheres. Even small children have their own television programming, addressing them in a special way. There is advertising and marketing from food products and toymakers aimed at children. Children have their own milieus: kindergarten and school environments. Youth culture has its own magazines, music, fashion, leisure activities, and so on. In many communities special teams are formed to prepare liturgies for children, teenagers, families. Communities cannot do without these specializations. The important point is to deepen the efforts of these groups who help people reflect on their faith in their families and with their children. Family catechesis and initiation in the sacraments must be linked with these efforts at deepening faith. Such initiatives of specialization and differentiation need help from professional sectors in the church to provide them with adequate materials suitable for families, young people, children, and so on. Well-trained people are needed for each of these milieus to help animate people who work with them. All this raises the question whether something different is needed to bring people together in Christian communities for conversion, nurture, and life in common.

Another very important area is that of different diaconal activities. The sick, the dying, the marginalized, those in need of counseling and guidance—in all these areas help is needed. In all these areas are a certain number of professional social workers. More and more deacons are moving into these areas. They try to assemble volunteers to work with them in and outside the communities. They put these volunteers in contact with professional social workers in order to get suitable instruction and the necessary knowledge to work in these fields. According to surveys in Germany, about one-third of the population are engaged in non-stipendiary activities. One million alone are in voluntary fire brigades, more than one million are in sports clubs, not to mention orchestras, choirs, and charitable societies. I am not speaking here merely of membership; these are also people taking on responsibilities. In all these areas there exists an institutionalized cooperation between volunteers and professionals. The latter provide formation, weekend courses, and the like. A similar cooperation between the German Catholic Charities and deacons, on one hand, and volunteers in the community, on the other hand, is still in the beginning phase. Such activities need to be presented more thoroughly in the public sphere.

A very important area for the presence of the community of the faithful in modern European society is in the major public dimensions of life. We need initiatives of Christians in the area of economics and the market, in the mass media, medicine and healthcare, politics, and so forth. There are, for example, groups of Christian politicians in Berlin who gather across party lines. There are groups of journalists who then choose their spiritual guide. Similar initiatives exist among professors at universities. Another area is that of theological education and formation at the various levels. It is interesting to see to what extent theological distance ("extension") learning is being utilized, and how theological study at the university level is being used by people who want more knowledge and a deepening of their faith.

The number of these newer forms for transmitting and proclaiming faith today is impressive. From these examples it should be clear how functional differentiation has a decisive impact on the lives of believers and the practice of their communities. To meet these needs the institutional features of the church need to be changed. And so we come to our final thesis.

Thesis 8
The form of the church as institution needs a fundamental revision. We need a flexible network of local and particular churches

*that respect the legitimate interests of the church-as-a-whole, and
of local and particular churches. The responsibility of the local
and particular churches must be reinforced. Only such a new
structure can open possibilities for the development of adequate
services and ministries in the church.*

In the first part of this presentation, I gave a general outline of
the erosion affecting the institutional structures of the church in
Europe. The faith cannot be proclaimed in a credible way if the
extreme Roman centralism continues to determine the shape of
the church. The flexible, differentiated structures of modern society require an adaptation of church structures and a distribution
of church authority. The directions of Vatican II have not yet been
taken seriously and explored in depth. A change in the centralism
in the church has not come about. Very similar is the situation of
bishops and bishops' conferences. At the parish level we experience how decision making is a process involving the parish priest,
the deacon, lay theologians, and the community through its representatives. Something similar should happen on the diocesan,
national, regional, continental, and universal levels. We have
helpful models of how this might be done in synodal structures
which should be revived. This can happen only if real decision-
making competence is given to the synods. It is not a dogma of
the church but an ideology that says that lay people can give
advice to bishops but that decision making belongs exclusively to
the hierarchy.

It is of greatest importance to reconsider the conditions for
admission to ecclesial ministry. Among the things needing recon-
sideration is the question of celibacy as a condition for priestly
ordination. Another important question is the admission of
women to the ordained diaconate. More than 75 percent of all
diaconal activity is the work of women. Moreover, the question
of admitting women to Holy Orders seems to me, theologically
speaking, to be open and, from a pastoral point of view, an
urgent issue. This does not mean that a decision in this matter
does not need time to mature. Perhaps the present course of
change will in time make the decisions seem less radical than they
do to traditionalists today. After all, we are witnessing whole new
approaches to pastoral and missionary work in modern Europe.
We have never had so many laity joining clergy and religious in

spiritual direction and in teaching. We have never had so many people engaged in diaconal activities. The whole image of the ministry is changing. It is time to give way to considering new forms of ministry to cope with the needs of the faithful and to meet the needs of men and women who are not now within the community of faith but who might enter it—if we Catholics found a way to reach out to them in ways appropriate to our times.

Response to Peter Hünermann

María Carmelita de Freitas, F.I.

PETER HÜNERMANN'S WELL-CONSTRUCTED, DIRECT, AND CLEAR language offers us abundant material for reflection and discussion. My comments on his paper come from my perspective as a Latin American woman.

The picture of the church in Europe today presented by Professor Hünermann and the challenges to evangelization it raises are indeed provocative. This was the case in the great truths he expressed in a serious and objective manner, encouraged by a prophetic boldness of the Holy Spirit; it was also true in the more indirect invitations throughout his presentation to continue imagining, "dreaming," and deepening from the rich soil of life, the daily living out of our faith as men and women committed to the God of the kingdom.

I will present my comments in the form of a theological parable, a gospel parable, and a symbol.

A Theological Parable

The parable of the clown of Kierkegaard, the nineteenth-century Danish theologian, is well known. Equally well known is the interpretation of that parable by Harvey Cox in his book *The Secular City*.[1] The parable is a simple one, taken from the daily life of peasant people. In a circus which had been set up in a small village, a fire broke out that threatened to destroy the circus and even the entire village. The circus owner was frightened and asked the first person who came along to alert the people about

---

[1] Harvey Cox, *The Secular City* (New York: Macmillan, 1966).

the danger and to get them to come help extinguish the blaze. That person was the clown, already dressed up for his role. The people interpreted the gestures and actions of the clown as a clever way of advertising the circus. They were amused by the clown and did not take the danger seriously. In the meantime, the fire spread and continued to consume everything in its path. Thus far the parable.

Harvey Cox compared the frustrated mission of the clown to the difficult ministry of theologians. Theologians try to get people's attention, warning them about changes and challenges they perceive to be flames on the horizon of the present and the future. For many their words appear to be exaggerations or trivial threats, lacking in professional seriousness and Christian spirit. Their talk is seen as part of a theologian's "character," saying what they have to say in order to fulfill their role, and their "character," internalized in the people's awareness, keeps the people from taking theologians seriously. Their role, like that of the biblical night watchman, who scans the horizon during the watches of the night, makes them vulnerable, a slate for writing contradictions. It is not uncommon that a theologian's message meets with indifference or, above all, the unavoidable resistance of those secure in their own truth.

The serious theological warnings we have heard in this presentation brought to mind Kierkegaard's parable and Cox's interpretation of it. When will the time arrive when the Catholic Church, as a European institution, will be ready to take seriously the signs of the present-day crisis? Will the church be prepared to abandon its security, so as to accept changes that are irreversible and require flexible positions and structures, designed to respond to completely different situations? In the same way, Hünermann's words reminded me of other "historic warnings," which today we consider as fulfilled prophecies. I am referring to two facts of the immediate pre–Vatican Council II period.

1. In the immediate postwar years, the pastoral letter of the Cardinal Archbishop of Paris *France: A Mission Country?* caused great controversy in situations even beyond Europe. In Brazil the bishops of that time, under the leadership of Dom Helder Câmara, were trying to organize their pastoral ministry in such a way as to enable collegiality and be a flexible response to the

signs of the times. The aforementioned text found resonance, arousing resistance on the one hand, and doubts and anxiety on the other. In other church settings the controversy was no doubt more intense, but in great part it proved to be fruitless. Was it not too much (as it was said at the time) to apply the name of "mission country" to the "favorite daughter of the church"? Even prescinding from the discussion about the meaning of the concept "mission" in that text, the truth of the matter was that countries of ancient Christian tradition were the first ones to "suffer" the effects of secularization, meaning "the process by which the institutions, actions and religious awareness lose their social meaning."[2] The statistics Hünermann presents give that pastoral text the quality of the fulfilled prophecy to which I referred earlier.

2. Before Vatican II, Karl Rahner began calling attention forcefully to the situation of *diaspora* in which Christianity found itself in the world, especially the Catholic Church.[3] The position he presented was the following: "Insofar as our outlook is really based on today and looking towards tomorrow, the present situation of Christians can be characterized as that of a diaspora; and this signifies, in terms of the history of salvation, a 'must,' from which we may and must draw conclusions about our behavior as Christians."[4] Rahner's point of departure was that the church found itself in a situation of diaspora in the whole world, and that this was a theological datum that was to be interpreted in the light of faith. For him,

the value set upon the Church in public life, in its medieval form, is not attributable, as a phenomenon, simply and solely to the supernatural power of the Church and Christianity. That particular form (not the Church's essential theological value) was also, at least in its factual existential

---

[2] R. B. Wilson, *La religione nel mondo contemporaneo* (Bologna: Il Mulino, 1985), 179.

[3] Karl Rahner, "The Present Situation of Christians: A Theological Interpretation of the Present Situation of Christians in the World," in *The Christian Commitment: Essays in Pastoral Theology* (New York: Sheed & Ward, 1963), 3-37.

[4] Ibid., 14.

realization, the result of temporal secular combinations of historical forces. It was a fact rather of cultural history than of theology.[5]

In 1972, the same author asked:

Do we at the same time think equally quickly and with the same concentration of how the Christian faith must be pro-claimed when it is no longer propped up by prevailing social realities? . . . Must we not adopt a spirit of self-criticism and resist a very dubious conservatism, which is becoming viru-lent as the euphoria of Vatican II is fading . . . ?[6]

In a situation of diaspora, of a little flock, one of the greatest risks which the church frequently has to run is the temptation of retiring to a "ghetto," closing in upon itself in a defensive man-ner, of reinforcing its external characteristics, structures, and institutions in a display of pseudo-security, avoiding any dia-logue. We have not heard here the word *diaspora*, but we have been able to identify some of the traits of the "warnings" of Rah-ner throughout the picture of the European church presented to us here.

With this I come to the central point of the impact which Hünermann's presentation made upon me and, based on this, to the questions I now ask as a Latin American, Brazilian, Christian woman: Would it not be a sign of maturity and sensitivity to the Spirit on the part of Latin American Christians, men and women, to reconsider and reread the profound "reading" of this presen-tation from the point of view of the reality in our countries and our Latin American churches? Basically, the old European "model," described here so clearly, was imposed upon us in the *Conquista,* reinforced by the laws of the *Patronado,* and is still, with few exceptions, in force in the majority of the particular churches, with only very slight modifications. However, aware-ness of that fact is less explicit for us today. Our people are rather

---

[5] Ibid., 21.
[6] Karl Rahner, *The Shape of the Church to Come* (London: SPCK, 1974), 27.

passive in relation to the ecclesiastical status quo, and religion still plays a fundamental role in the collective and social picture. But the signs of the crisis are now becoming visible, with greater or less intensity depending on the context. Will we be sufficiently lucid and humble to grasp such signs and their possible consequences? Will we be sufficiently bold to help bring about the changes that are coming upon us?

In a recent article on the situation of the Catholic Church, theologian Clodovis Boff affirms that the "frontier of ecclesial vitality shifted after Vatican II from the North to the South of the world. . . . But the administrative center of the Church is not there where life is lived."[7] This has not only caused conflicts, but continues to do so. In the same text, the author notes the existence of two projects in tension in the church: one of recentralization of power and one of grass-roots participation. For him, in a manner very similar to Hünermann's mentioning of what of the "new" is arising, it is necessary to insist on

> the proposal of a participative Church. Such a proposal is based on the New Testament: it represents Jesus' dream; it follows the ecclesial practice of the first Christians; it was the normative and normal practice of the entire ancient Church; it is backed by the best of Vatican II; it is the most appropriate model for modern times, sensitive to the yearning for freedom and participation.[8]

One can ask, therefore: To what extent is such a model being implemented in our particular churches? Will we be ready to learn from the experience of the countries of ancient Christian tradition? What are we doing so that the future of our ecclesial communities might respond to the new interventions of the Spirit in an effective manner, to the new signs of the times? What can religious life do, and what should it do, to support and make this "model" more effective?

---

[7] Clodovis Boff, "Uma análise de conjuntura da igreja católica no final do milênio," *Revista Eclesiastica Brasileira* 221 (March 1996): 126-30.

[8] Ibid., 148.

A Gospel Parable

Here is the place for the Gospel parable I mentioned at the beginning. I refer to the parable of the crippled woman in Luke 13:10ff. The woman had been for many years under the power of an evil spirit and had been made ill. She was bent over and could not stand up straight at all. She could not raise her head to look at a distance, to see the world and reality from a different and broader point of view. Her horizon was limited to a few meters of the ground in front of her. Jesus finds her in the synagogue, on the Sabbath, and frees her. Straightening up with dignity, the woman realizes that the burden which had oppressed her had been removed, that the world is very different from what she had thought it to be, that broad extensive spaces of freedom and movement were opened before her as a challenge and an invitation to enter upon new and unknown paths.

This parable from the Gospel throws much light on the crucial question under consideration here: the church as institution, whether in Europe or in other contexts, has to let go of the obstacles of inadequate structures, which maintain the church's inertia and incapacity to move. They prevent the church from being the salvific presence in the world, the mission in the diaspora, an audible and credible Word in the new areopagus of today's society. It is necessary that the church set loose the living forces that are bound by obsolete laws or concepts, so as to be free and able to act in the common mission of all baptized persons, men and women.

A Symbol

Finally, a symbol. We Christians from various churches, and also non-Christians from different religions, are celebrating at this time (and not only in Latin America) the twentieth anniversary of the martyrdom of Oscar Romero, the bishop who was murdered because he defined the life of the poor. Romero was not born a friend and defender of the poor. He made himself "friend" and defender of the poor via a long and painful road of conversion. It was from that experience that the compelling force came which Romero had in his life and in his death. The Dogmatic Constitution on the Church, *Lumen Gentium*, tells us that the church is a pilgrim church, an *ecclesia semper reformanda*, always on the road to conversion. Let us hope that the church can hold up the memory of such saints of the institution as Oscar Romero throughout the whole world—setting out, with the help of the Spirit, on the rocky road of conversion that is called for in our new times.

5

The Mission of Religious Men and Women in Latin America Today

A Liberating Mission in a Neoliberal World

María Carmelita de Freitas, F.I.

GAUDIUM ET SPES, THE PASTORAL CONSTITUTION ON THE Church in the Modern World of Vatican II, tells us that if questions are to be fruitful, they must be formulated from a specific situation and time. In line with this, I want to share my reflection on my own situation as a Latin American woman of consecrated life in this time of neoliberal Latin America. Starting with the presupposition that this is a historically situated reflection, I will focus my topic and its questions from the perspective of the missionary "itinerancy" of Jesus, having as a background the incident of his conversation with the Samaritan woman (John 4:1-42). This story in the Gospel of John has an extraordinary beauty and has a clear missionary significance in its dialogical, liberative, and countercultural character. Permit me to recall its main lines: under the hot midday sun, Jesus arrives, tired and thirsty, at Sychar and sits down next to Jacob's well, a place charged with memories for his people. A Samaritan woman, carrying her jar, comes to the well to draw water. Going against the rigid customs of the society of his time, Jesus engages her in a conversation, transforming his initial request into an offer of living water. With extraordinary respect, this unknown Jew enters into the secret of that anonymous life of one who had suffered so much and, little by little, brings her to open herself to the revelation of her reality as someone who is excluded—because she was a woman, a Samaritan, and for not having a husband. Her openness to that liberating revelation of her identity leads her to the surprising revelation of the messianic identity of the one speaking with her, who leads her from the ancestral source of water (Jacob's well) to the divine source of water: "Believe me, woman, the hour has come in which neither on this mountain, nor in Jerusalem will you adore the Father." The disciples approach, not understanding the sublime character of that moment. The woman, urged by the movement of the Spirit, leaves her jar, goes down to the city, and becomes a missionary to her people. Jesus extends his gaze to see the golden harvest ready to be gathered in, and teaches the disciples. The Samaritans, drawn by the word of the woman, arrive as the firstfruits of that historical-eschatological, divine harvest.

My concern here is not the exegesis of this Johannine text. Rather—unlike the disciples who did not wish to ask any questions—we are going to ask about the meaning of the mission of Latin American men and women religious today in a neoliberal world. This basic question will be heard throughout this reflection. Following the internal dynamics of the text (John 4:1-42), this presentation will be developed in three parts: (1) the postconciliar journey of religious life in Latin America: liberating mission as a hermeneutical key; (2) the mission of religious life in Latin America in a neoliberal world: prophetic resistance and solidarity; (3) mission in the perspective of the future: witnesses of the kingdom and signs of hope.

The Postconciliar Journey of Religious Life in Latin America—Liberating Mission as a Hermeneutical Key

Jesus, wearied with the journey, sat down beside the well. It was about the sixth hour. There came a woman from Samaria to draw water and Jesus said to her: "Give me to drink. . . . If you knew the gift of God and who it is that is saying to you . . . you would ask him and he would give you living water." (John 4:6, 7, 10)

A *Pilgrimage in Faith*

The Second Vatican Council called religious men and women to undertake a journey: to journey with the pilgrim People of God, to live an experience of profound renewal, to go back to the source of "living water" from where every genuinely Christian religious experience takes its origin and is nourished. As was the case for the entire church, that call also moved religious life to a new understanding of its identity and mission in the world. If what was most visible in that movement was the search for what was new (new practices, new theological foundations, new forms of expression), that quest was also animated by a spirit of returning to the evangelical roots or origin of religious life: a return to the "Gospel as criterion and fundamental norm," to the sources of the founding charisms, animated above all by the conviction that the time of the Spirit had come, a new *kairos* of God for his people.

The changes that took place in response to the call of the council were oriented in two different directions: toward presence in the modern and secularized world, and toward the particular church as the Christian community in the world. As happened to the Samaritan woman, religious life in its postconciliar pilgrimage found God, the Source of Living Water, in a place where it would have been considered improbable years before—in the world, in the midst of daily life and its activities. The first attempts to renew community and apostolic life came out of this encounter, especially for women's congregations. It was a question above all of an institutional renewal and *ad intra*, giving priority to the *reforms* in the organization of the community, in the relationship of authority and obedience, in forms of living and expressing both the vows and mission in the modern context of that time.

Just as Jesus' conversation with the Samaritan woman made her abandon her accustomed path and made her aware of her truth and opened her to new horizons of life and impelled her into mission, so too the efforts to return to the roots or origin of religious life upset the balance of "normality" to which religious life had become accustomed, and opened the way for questioning and self-criticism and the inevitable identity crisis. At that point began the disintegration of the concept of religious life as it had been historically understood, which was the prelude to changes heretofore considered unthinkable or impossible for religious life as a whole. The theologian José Comblin, referring to those efforts at renewal, said: "those communities did not know what they wanted, but knew very well what they did not want."[1] That is, community and mission structures were rejected because they were considered less and less adequate for the historical moment in which they were living.

The more substantial elements in this process of change immediately after the council could be said to have been common to religious life as a whole and worldwide. As time went on, this process was more intense in the countries of the so-called First World, since they were affected more strongly by the phenomenon of secularization. In Latin America, because of the particular socioeconomic, political, and ecclesial conditions of the continent, the process had other specific qualities, especially beginning with Medellín and Puebla.

In fact, the original and creative reception of the council on the continent was manifest in a pluriform way, affecting the life of the church in all its dimensions. Basic Ecclesial Communities (BECs) multiplied all over the continent, opening spaces for living out faith in profound relation to life, from a perspective of liberation, and a growing appropriation of the Word of God. The great contradictions in the socioeconomic system of the time proved to be clearly incapable of rectifying the social imbalance and producing the urgent changes that were necessary. Politically, the establishment of authoritarian regimes in several countries, with arbitrary rules and repression, changed abruptly the political and social scene of the continent, and had repercussions for the direction the church was taking. These governments' prohibition of many of the new social and pastoral initiatives of the church led the church to take bold and prophetic steps denouncing such moves. The yearning of the people for liberation found support and encouragement in the BECs, in concrete pastoral activities, in an engaged religious life, and in the theology of lib-

---

[1] José Comblin, "Significado das Pequenas Comunidades," *Convergência* 58 (January-February 1972): 104.

eration that emerged in those years to great affirmation. At the end of the 1970s, in spite of the complex climate that had developed, Puebla confirmed and legitimated the major intuitions and advances of that period, and gave official approbation to a liberating evangelization under the aegis of the preferential option for the poor. From that time onward, a theological trend of thought specific and original to Latin America had been formed.

Under such circumstances, by journeying with the believing and poor people of God, religious men and women became more aware of a world that is tired and thirsty—in which there are seeds of death and of life, where there is a growing gap between rich and poor, where there is marginalization, division, and exclusion based on culture, race, gender, social class, and religion. Thus began a genuine historical turn in religious life toward the "nether world" of the poor, with its questions and challenges. The acute need for urgent and profound structural changes, experienced at all levels and in all dimensions (including the internal life of the church) gave the process a distinctively Latin American stamp, which was legitimated and supported by Medellín. The reallocation of religious (especially religious women) to the "nether world" of the poor began rather timidly at the time, but received explicit acknowledgment: "Those communities who feel themselves called to form, among its members, small communities truly incarnated in a poor milieu: receive our encouragement."[2]

The Conference of Latin American Religious (CLAR), in fidelity to the spirit of Medellín, exhorted, "We religious should enter more determinedly into the work of human promotion . . . allocating a greater percentage of personnel toward the field and other centers for the marginalized and manifesting an effective preference for the poor."[3] Concern for knowing and analyzing the sociocultural and ecclesial reality gained ground and consistency in particular sectors of religious life. Even as efforts were being made to incorporate theoretical elements into those analyses so as to make them objective and credible, religious men and

---

[2] Second Latin American Episcopal Conference, *Documento sobre la Pobreza* (Medellín, 1968), no. 16.

[3] Conference of Latin American Religious (CLAR), *Misión del Religioso en America Latina* (Bogotá: CLAR, 1969), no. 5.

women, as they were developing critical consciousness, were confronted with the situations of structural injustice existing in society, oftentimes legitimated by the pastoral practice of the church. Engaged religious life as a phenomenon helped form a more radical expression of option for the poor.

This experience of engagement resulted in the concrete and historical discovery of the multiethnic and multicultural reality of the continent, which led religious life to what has been called the fourth dimension of the *exodus* of religious life to the periphery—the *cultural exodus*. Indeed, for many religious, especially religious women, who had been directed toward this engagement beginning in the 1970s, this was a surprising and challenging affirmation: the indigenous peoples, the poor, those in rural areas or in the outlying areas of the great urban peripheral zones possessed their own culture, their own ways of being religious, their own symbolic worlds. A rich and complex cultural world existed there, at once unknown and under threat, as a challenge and as a place of *mission*. Religious men and women gradually became aware that, in order to take up that challenge of cultural pluralism, an authentic and continuous process of conversion was necessary to overcome senses of cultural superiority and prejudice that had roots centuries old. They also realized that even as they themselves were channels of the living water which God was offering to the poor, religious life was receiving living water from them. The gift was reciprocal. Journeying together with the poor, an authentic *Latin American* form of religious life was being shaped. Religious men and women were learning anew in their daily lives to share the hope, the sorrows, and the anxieties of this world, acknowledging it as the site of history and cultures where the kingdom of God had to be established. Their place was within this site as servants of the kingdom of God, as disciples of Jesus who were being sent so that all may have life. In that world they received the living water of the Spirit and they shared it with brothers and sisters of different cultures and races.

New questions were being addressed to religious life. For example, what does it mean to allow oneself to be evangelized by the poor? How can we evangelize from the perspective of the poor? How can we live out justice and solidarity in a society that is structurally unjust? How can we accept the inevitable conflict coming to those who live in solidarity with the poor? How can we be agents of a holistic liberation? How can we break with and form a new relationship to the past? Put simply: How can we as religious be one with the poor of the earth? These questions challenge not only engaged communities, but also (albeit indirectly) all forms of religious life.

Today it is very clear that the postconciliar journey of religious life in Latin America was extremely fruitful. It led to the rediscovery of the privileged place of the poor in the kingdom, religious life's identity as situated in history, its prophetic voice, its radically ecclesial dimension or, put another way, its Christian vocation in the world. And it is also a very clear awareness that mission is the principal hermeneutical key in this journey.

Mission as a Hermeneutical Key

A little before Puebla, CLAR affirmed that today mission constitutes "the key for understanding the charism of religious life. The awareness of being-for-mission becomes ever clearer for us. . . . It could truly be said that a new awareness of mission and a very special sensitivity to its demands motivated and set in motion that most significant processes of change which took place in religious life."[4] Indeed, if one analyzes the paths taken, it is clear that mission is the key point of reference for explaining the principal lines of development. It was through the spaces provided by mission that religious men and women entered more and more into the local church, into society, into the "netherworld" of the poor and the excluded, into indigenous cultures, into the new "areopagoi" and from there interpreted their own self-understanding of their Christian vocation. CLAR also affirmed that "[r]eligious life in Latin America today is being reinterpreted and is being understood from the point of view of mission."

This new self-understanding on the basis of mission, of being radically sent in service to the world, placed us on the threshold of an unprecedented point in the history of religious life on the continent, characterized by a keen, critical consciousness—apparently irreversible—of the role of religious life in the historical

---

[4] CLAR, *Tendencias proféticas de la Vida Religiosa en America Latina* (Bogotá: CLAR, n.d.), no. 24, p. 27.

construction of society, as well as its specific mission to that society. That reinterpretation of the practice (and practices) of religious life based on mission had as its theoretical point of reference the *new theology* of mission that had been developing since the first decades of the twentieth century and found great resonance at the Second Vatican Council.

With its ecclesiology of the People of God (*Lumen Gentium*), its emphasis on the presence of the church in the world (*Gaudium et Spes*), and with the new perspectives on mission it tried to put forth, Vatican II created the basis for rethinking the mission of the church in the modern and postmodern world. Paul VI's *Evangelii Nuntiandi* confirmed and extended the perspectives of the council. Later (1990), the document "Dialogue and Proclamation" of the Pontifical Council for Interreligious Dialogue moved further, opening unprecedented perspectives, especially in relation to ecumenical and interreligious dialogue. To be sure, all of this had great repercussions in the theology of religious life. The council itself insisted on overcoming the ancient dichotomy of consecration and mission of the preconciliar theology of religious life.

At the same time, especially in Europe, postconciliar theology developed a powerful synthesis of the principal conciliar and postconciliar insights into mission: the trinitarian origin of mission; the kingdom of God (announced by Jesus Christ and present in history by the power of the Spirit) as horizon and goal of being missionary in the church; baptism as a gift of salvation that calls us into mission; the different dimensions of mission—proclamation (*Lumen Gentium* 5), promotion of justice (*Gaudium et Spes* 41; Synod of Bishops [1971]), inculturation and prophetic-transformative presence in the world (*Evangelii Nuntiandi*), interreligious dialogue (*Redemptoris Missio*), and the subject of the signs of the times. All this led to changing the understanding of mission as what the church *does*, into making it clear that mission is the very *being* itself of the church, as affirmed by Vatican II: "The pilgrim church is missionary by her very nature. For it is from the mission of the Son and the mission of the Holy Spirit that she takes her origin, in accordance with the decree of God the Father" (*Ad Gentes* 2). "The mission of the church, therefore, is fulfilled by that activity which makes her fully present to all men and nations . . . leading them to faith, freedom and the peace of God" (*Ad Gentes* 5).

In Latin America, Medellín and Puebla acted as catalysts for that reflection and promoters of the ecclesial dynamism that accompanied it. The emphasis Medellín placed on the signs of the times constituted, according to some, a new paradigm or model of mission, the incarnational paradigm. The scandal of poverty on the continent was seen as one of the clearest signs of the times challenging Christian consciousness and mission for the entire ecclesial community. The preferential option for the poor was precisely an effort to respond to that sign of the times, according to the gospel of Jesus and from the perspective of the privileged place of the poor in the kingdom.

By the same token, with the progress of the human sciences and their impact on theology, the category of *history*, so typical of modern thought, came to find ample space in postconciliar theological discussion, requiring theologians to reconsider many positions and formulations considered until that time definitive. It was clear that any reference to history and to a specific historical context leads us, from a Christian perspective, inevitably to the theme of mission, understood as being radically sent as a Christian, as a religious, in service to the world.

The concept of mission that undergirded the traditional theology of religious life and its practices was radically reformulated, overcoming the anachronistic dichotomy between identity and mission (i.e., doing apostolic work) that was typical of preconciliar religious life. An acute awareness grew among religious men and women that religious life cannot be considered and conceived of as an entity in itself, shut up in its own essence and defined in an a priori manner, once and for all in some ahistorical form. The tendency of previous epochs to define the identity of religious life in an a priori and universal manner and then to apply it to a concrete situation was overcome. The big question was no longer what religious life was. Rather, it was about the meaning of being a religious today in a specific sociohistorical and ecclesial context. This meant moving decisively toward a more descriptive, inductive theology, rethinking the identity of religious life as something situated historically. As theologian Carlos Palacio put it, "The inherent risks in transposing identity into historical categories are not greater than those which threaten religious life when it allows itself to be paralysed by a predefined—and there-fore ossified and abstract—identity."[5]

Thus, an abstract and disembodied concept of identity gave way to a dynamic perception of identity, that is, one in intrinsic and radical reference to history, in relationship to the "other," who is present and challenges us in this historical context. On the Latin American continent today, that other is above all those who are poor, marginalized, and excluded. They become for religious life its *theological locus;* they provoke its exodus toward the mar-gins of the current systems, toward the desert, the frontier, and the periphery.

Indeed, the most characteristic and radical evangelical dimen-sion in all this postconciliar process of Latin American religious life was, no doubt, the *preferential option for the poor.* The new forms of presence of the poor in society, their relationship to a socioeconomic context marked by injustice and inequality led religious, especially religious women, to an experience of *decen-tering*, that is to say, moving from the center to the periphery, toward the "netherworld"of the poor, as a new way of living mis-sion in the following of Jesus.

At the beginning of the 1990s, CLAR explained the theologi-cal meaning of that exodus and its consequences:

> The exodus of religious life, like that of the BEC's, toward the poor and the periphery is a displacement of interests and options. The option is for a new understanding of self: to see history from the point of view of the poor and the little ones (Luke 1:51) and to reinterpret one's own identity from them. . . . Accepting that challenge, religious life maintains its fidelity to the God of Jesus and, at the same time, rediscov-ers its prophetic power and its evangelical and martyrial vocation. It is not simply a question of a pastoral strategy; it is an understanding of self which touches one's own identity. The theological fact of the incarnation, of the kenosis, illu-mines and clarifies the steps and stages of this process.[6]

---

[5] Carlos Palacio, *Reinterpretar a vida religiosa* (São Paulo: Paulinas, 1991), 62.

[6] CLAR, *Subsidio para los delegados(as) de la vida religiosa a Santo Domingo: SSV Junta Directiva* (Costa Rica, June 1992), p. 2.

That experience led to the affirmation of the option for the poor as having very deep roots in the charism and history of each religious institute, and this helped many congregations to go back to their sources for a new reading of their origins.

In this decentering toward a suffering people—a new historical version of the Suffering Servant—religious life immersed itself in the great prophetic current of the little ones and the oppressed. In doing this it retrieved all this biblical image's symbolic power, becoming a parable in action, showing the church and society what is means to anticipate in a real and prefiguring manner the utopia of the kingdom, precisely in those places where life is being threatened. And it is also in this way that it comes to know the experience of martyrdom.

Today it is possible to grasp better the importance of this profound theological and evangelical option. The engagement of the poor in their own geographical location had led to a change of social and cultural place. From there has arisen the necessity for inculturation. New spaces of presence in the political world have opened in being part of popular movements and in the field of human rights. There is greater collaboration with the laity, with organizations and institutions (ecclesial and otherwise) who are concerned with the situation of increasing poverty in the world. There has been greater awareness of the dignity of the religious woman in society and in the church. The presence of religious men and women among indigenous people and among black people has become greater. Indigenous forms of religious life have come into being, and vocations from among the common people increased in number. New forms of ecumenical collaboration also arose in defense of human rights of the poor and the excluded. In this movement of religious life it is possible to discern "a sign of the times, a clear presence of the Spirit in the present-day history of humanity, a sign of the passage, of the Paschal Mystery of the Lord in the midst of his people, a place from which the Spirit speaks to his church."[7]

However, there is a way of reading that exodus of religious life to the poor which sees only what is more visible and, therefore, more superficial and even anecdotal. Such a reading cannot give

---

[7] Ibid., 2.

an account of the ultimate and theological meaning of this phenomenon. In order to respond to the question in that sense, one must proceed in another way, by reading what is more utterly central and irreducible in it: the great passion for the God of the poor, and the determined will to follow Jesus, the one who reveals that God of the poor, and to continue his liberating mission. The theological point of reference in all of this process is the *Incarnation*. The experience of *kenosis*, of learning-to-be in history, through suffering and obedience, what one already is *in nuce*, is a constitutive element of Christian experience and an inescapable one for religious life.

In the postconciliar journey, the religious woman, like the Samaritan woman, is invited to open herself to a new perspective of life and mission, to be sensitive to the presence of the Spirit in history, to listen to his voice, which is sounding everywhere, and to take on the liberating mission of Jesus, as witness of the kingdom in the midst of her people.

The Mission of Religious Life in a Neoliberal World– Prophetic-Countercultural Resistance and Solidarity

How is it that you, a Jew, ask a drink of me, a woman of Samaria? . . . Just then his disciples came. They marveled that he was talking with a woman. . . . So the woman left her water jar, and went away into the city. (John 4:9, 27-32)

Exclusion for social-religious reasons was a fact that affected the life of Samaritans, especially of Samaritan women. Jesus knew this, but did not exclude them from the sphere of his life and of his mission. He spoke with the woman, revealed God's mysteries to her, introduced her into the dynamic of the kingdom, and sent her out on mission, by the gift of the Spirit. Jesus' attitude calls into question all our latent or manifest forms of discrimination and exclusion.

In Latin American society today the phenomenon of exclusion becomes every day more evident and dramatic, oppressing like a dead weight the backs of the poor under the aegis of neoliberal globalization. It has become worse since the beginning of the 1980s, as a result of the great impact of the rigid enforcement and extension of neoliberal economic policies, which have caused the conditions of life for people in Latin America to deteriorate more and more. The social fabric, increasingly affected by the omnipresence of neoliberal globalization, is becoming ever weaker, more fragmented and divided.

Without bypassing the complexity of this question, nor intending to make definitive judgments about it, it is necessary to recognize that the present-day system is one that is characteristically atomizing and excluding. Some of the characteristic component elements of this system affect, with a cruel realism, the life of ever-growing sectors of our peoples. I wish to call attention to some of them. First of all, *the religion of the market*. In the transnational economy of current neoliberalism, defined by high levels of monetary flow rather than by the flow of goods and services,[8] real economic power is exercised by anonymous uncontrolled financial markets, which ignore geographical boundaries and take on the character of omnipresent power, introducing the future into present time in an unprecedented manner. They are like divine attributes, which give way to a new religion, the religion of the market.[9] In this new religion human lives are subordinated to the interests of the market, conferring on the latter an absolute character. Let us examine several aspects of this neoliberalism.

First, the *neoliberal creed*, or the fetish of the indicators of monetary and economic stability. The obsessive insistence on stability contains within it a deceit that can easily alienate consciousness. It is so transformed into the best apology possible for the system against any type of criticism of the fallacies of economic development based fundamentally on the accumulation and unequal distribution of wealth. Inoculating the general population with this fetish through the mass media ends up engendering a confused but growing adherence to the neoliberal creed, enslaving consciousness and paralyzing initiatives.

Second, the *ethics of efficiency*. The market does not accept

---

[8] Inázio Neutzling, "A grande transformação socio-econômica do capitalismo no final do século XX: Algunas características," *Convergência* no. 293 (June 1996): 325.

[9] Ibid., 326.

losers. In order not to lose, it is necessary to be efficient. The behavior of persons and of social groups is then subordinated to the market, which then defines the sense of life and of human reality. The only possible and desirable ethic in such a situation is that of efficiency. Outside efficiency there is no law or justice.

Third, the *gospel of competition*. This new gospel proclaims that competitive engagement in the international market is the only possible way to salvation. Competition so understood and practiced increases exasperation, individualism, legitimates a social Darwinism decked out with new scientific appurtenances, and inculcates the logic of war, whether in the relationship among the corporations or in the behavior of social actors—in the public sector, in the financial sector, in schools, in the university, or in the religious sector.[10]

The obvious consequence of all of this is the *logic of exclusion*, which is considered by many to be the principal or major fact of our times. As the preparatory document of the Twelfth General Assembly of CLAR observes:

> It is a question of something more serious than the reduction of resources in the social sector. It is the abandonment of the poor to themselves, the lack of commitment on the part of the State to the social sector. In that way, neoliberalism throws the great majority of the population of the planet onto the trash heap.[11]

For the ecclesial consciousness of Latin America, this principal fact of social exclusion constitutes an unprecedented challenge: How to take a stand before the neoliberal globalized face of our contemporary world? How to continue to encourage the least ones on the earth, giving them hope, when one is aware that the historical liberations for which they fought and died in the decades from the 1960s to the 1980s are always farther away in the horizon of peoples and nations? And if one wants to pretend that "outside the market there is no salvation" or that "we have

---

[10] Inázio Neutzling, "A crise da modernidade brasileira e os desafios para a via religiosa," *Convergência* no. 290 (March 1996): 99.

[11] CLAR, "Texto introductorio a la XII Asemblea General de la CLAR," *Boletín CLAR* 35 no. 2 (1997): 81.

arrived at the end of history," what does it mean to continue the mission of Jesus and to reaffirm the priority of the poor in the kingdom? In such a historical circumstance, mission has peculiar requirements. Among them are prophetic and countercultural resistance and solidarity that is human, macro-ecumenical, and ecological in nature.

Prophetic and Countercultural Resistance

It is not possible to be sent in mission by the God of life and then make a deal with situations of death or to be compliant with systems or mechanisms that engender them. The Jesuit provincial superiors of Latin America said the following about this situation:

> Before this reality which contradicts the work of the Creator, the demand of faith, so that God may be God among us, consists in resisting the dynamics which destroy our brothers and sisters and, in working with many others in order to change the present situation, assured that in this way we are contributing to the construction of a society which is closer to the kingdom proclaimed by Jesus Christ.[12]

If it is not possible to stop the advancement of globalization or of the market and its inexorable laws with useless laments and voluntary actions, that does not necessarily mean that we accept that we have arrived at the end of history and at the death of utopias. If the frameworks we have used up till now do not succeed in explaining the novelty and complexity of the situation, we will have to be humble and creative in seeking out other points of reference or models that will allow us to continue to advance, even though there may be no great certainty. If the means which served as tools to build a path of liberation in previous decades show themselves today to be insufficient, we will have to discover, critically and patiently, new ways of analyzing and of act-

---

[12] Provincial Superiors of the Society of Jesus in Latin America, "O neoliberalismo na America Latina" (São Paulo, 1996), no. 39, 27.

ing in order that the mission of religious life might not lose its prophetic and countercultural sense, nor cease to encourage creative resistance among the least among us. In the 1970s and 1980s the biblical paradigm of the exodus inspired and enlightened mission, especially of communities engaged in the midst of the people, among the poor. Today, as Victor Codina's words dramatically capture, the horizon in which we live is more similar to Babylon—the greatest crisis in the history of the People of God— when the empire of Babylon was the absolute lord of everything:

> "In all things I will always be queen. I am, and there is no other" (Is 47:7-8). The silent but creative and persistent resistance of the remaining few, of the *anawim,* becomes paradigmatic for mission today. Without losing sight of the horizon of utopia, it will be necessary to begin with the micro, the small. That of everyday life . . . it will be necessary to recover the importance of the daily grind of life and to take advantage of the small liberations . . . go from exodus to exile. Continue following the footsteps of the Servant of Yahweh . . . rediscovering the dimension of the Paschal Mystery and of the Spirit.[13]

From this point of view, two attitudes seem to be particularly necessary: (1) *Humility without easy concessions.* The time in which we are living is obviously not one of great certainty, and this obliges us to review our attitudes, rethink our models, paradigms, and strategies just as the People of God did during the exile. But this does not excuse us from continuing to carry forward the mission of Jesus and the cause of the poor along paths which perhaps are now more bold, prophetic, and countercultural than those trodden till now, according to how the Spirit leads us. (2) *Clarity without dogmatism.* It is necessary to know how to discern the new signs of the times, without giving in to the temptation of repeating models, imposing prescriptions, or absolutizing conquests of other historical moments. Dialogue, personal and corporate search, and the courage to believe in the God of the

---

[13] Victor Codina, "Cultura e inculturación" (mimeographed, 1999), p. 22.

kingdom beyond all apparent historical failures are requirements of such a clarity of mind, which allows us to be critical and constructive in the new situations which afflict our people.

Human, Cosmic, and Ecological Solidarity

From the point of view of the gospel, it is clear that the distance between the project of Jesus and the project of neoliberal globalization becomes greater every day. The evil effects of this worldwide system have already affected millions of persons and whole populations. The seriousness of the problem is undeniable, and it is urgent that relationships of solidarity be promoted in all sectors of society as an alternative to growing individualism. In his annual allocution to the Diplomatic Corps in January 2000, Pope John Paul II was most categorical: "The century which is opening before us has to be one of solidarity."

In Christian revelation, solidarity is a basic datum that has deep roots in the experience of Israel and permeates the entirety of the message of Jesus. The gratuitous love and solidarity of God for the human person—created in God's image and likeness—and for the whole of creation is an unmistakable and persistent element of revelation. The God of biblical revelation is a God of solidarity, who calls the people to solidarity and denounces the lack of solidarity among the people. The prophets as spokespersons of Yahweh reel against all forms of oppression and exploitation, against accumulation which generates division and exclusions, since what God desires is justice and solidarity, not theft, violations of rights and false sacrifices (cf. Amos 5:21). Through their preaching, they attempt to keep alive the commitment to the poor, and to denounce abuses that result from accumulated wealth in detriment to the little ones and those living in misery (Amos 5:7-11; Micah 3:1-4). They cry out against the injustices committed against the humble, because this is against the covenant, and breaks the ideal of communion with God and of solidarity with the problems of the community (Jer. 31:29-30). The Incarnation of the Son of God is the most complete expression of the solidarity of the God of the covenant with sinful humanity. This fundamental solidarity of God is the horizon within which Jesus of Nazareth engages his whole life and mission, and which permits him to be characterized as the man for others.

If the biblical revelation of God, culminating in Jesus of Nazareth, is mercy and solidarity made concrete in being in favor of the life of the poor, in loving tenderly those who are excluded from history and from the banquet of life, in identifying oneself with the victims of this world, then what does it mean to take seriously all this in a society that insists on ignoring and denying the primacy of the human person above all other goods? How can this conviction be made transparent? How can this revelation be made credible? How can we give historical plausibility to the commitment to a God who is a God of solidarity? How are we to understand the evangelical imperative of solidarity?

In the dramatic situation in which humanity is immersed, and in light of the Word of God, it is unavoidable that the concern for the project of a society of solidarity renders the Christian conscience restless and raises radical questions concerning our way of conceiving the commitment to the gospel and to the mission of Jesus. We are celebrating two thousand years of the Incarnation of the Word, and we are still trying to decipher that what it means for the mission of the ecclesial community to be incarnated is to become real flesh in *real* history.

From this point of view, solidarity cannot be reduced to a mere abstract notion or to an ideal, capable of making eloquent speeches but sterile at the level of practices and of commitment. Charity that does not go beyond the sporadic or routine giving of alms, and which acts as a tranquilizer for individual or collective conscience cannot be considered more than a palliative, legitimating a comfortable position, without any transforming effects on the status quo. Supposed neutrality before grave or serious social problems, under the guise of universal solidarity, is another way of distorting the commandment of love, of solidarity. The word of Jesus is incisive: "either with me or against me." As John Paul II said in a speech to La Comisión Económica para América Latina (CEPAL) in Santiago de Chile: "It is not only a question of the profession of good intentions, but of a decided commitment to seek effective solutions in the technical field of economy, with the farsightedness which love gives and the creativity which springs from solidarity."

It can be said that the anguished perception of the need of life for all, experienced at the world level, based on the principles of a universal and even cosmic and ecological solidarity, certainly constitutes one of the most unmistakable and urgent signs of the times. It is a requirement of God's project for humanity. It is the foundation of all humans living together, and it affects all the aspects and spaces of that life. Its goal is clear: consolidating unity of the great human family weakened by divisions and discriminations originating from multiple causes. "It is a question of carrying out concretely the series of material, spiritual, and religious conditions which will allow all the members of society . . . to reach levels of a life compatible with human dignity."[14] The Synod of Bishops for America placed in evidence the need for global solidarity which embraces the different regions and human and spiritual realities of the whole continent. From that point of view, the construction of a society of solidarity necessarily has to move today through the demolition of all barriers or forms of discrimination, division, and segregation, including those of a religious nature, which so deeply mark today's world.

Those barriers which prevent solidarity today have concrete names. They include insufficient awareness among the citizenry, resulting from numerous historical or structural causes. They include the relationships of gender, ancient barriers that will not be overcome without the effective participation of men and women. They include the social distances among the races. Only the true perception of the fundamental dignity of the person and of her rights (independent of her ethnic or racial origin) and a determined courage to create universal solidarity beyond those differences breach that wall, frequently identified as the wall of shame, of ignominy, of apartheid. They include the divisions among Christians and among the different religions, which today provoke the greatest scandal and make the credible proclamation of the gospel more difficult, as well as the historical plausibility of the church. There is the cruel and anti-solidarity aggression against the environment, against the dwelling place of all things and all people, the "common house" (*oikos*), which today constitutes an extremely serious barrier, because that aggression is made in favor of a few, and it penalizes the great majority of the world's population, besides risking the survival of the whole of

---

[14] National Conference of Brazilian Bishops, "Exigéncias éticas da ordem politica" (1989), no. 82.

humanity. A vision of solidarity of the world, an ethics of solidarity and an effective coresponsibility of the common weal are some of the ways of overcoming this. The planetary dimensions of such solidarity indicate the gravity and scope of this cause. To struggle for this is to be in solidarity with the defense and protection of life—all forms of life—and to broaden the horizons of solidarity beyond the limits of the human condition.

Challenged by all of this, religious life finds itself today in need of rethinking its way of being present and of carrying out its mission in the world. Solidarity is a basic component of the origin of religious life in the church, and of the origin of the different foundational charisms. In the origin of each congregation or religious institute, the evangelical intuition of solidarity, particularly with the poor and those excluded from the social order, is always present, in one form or other. This attitude must be assumed today with renewed consciousness and decision. Inactivity cannot be justified because of the complexity of the mechanisms which engender or bring about this challenge. Rather, it is necessary to look today for new forms of commitment, that are capable of articulating a project of solidarity based on the victims of the system.

It seems that the efforts that are being made in this regard in Latin America are directed in three different directions, and that these open perspectives for the future. The first dimension is at the very heart of religious life. Here the creative fidelity of religious life to its vocation and mission in present-day situations enters into play. From this point of view, the only possible attitude is, without doubt, the clear affirmation of the absolute character of the kingdom of God, and the radical reference to the mission and practices of Jesus. Before the pretensions of the definitive character of the religion of the market, with its laws of competitiveness and the idols of efficiency and consumerism, it is necessary to reaffirm with words and, above all, by the witness of life, both personal and collective, that God alone is absolute, that the kingdom of God is the principal reference point for human life together, and for the non-negotiable centrality of life and of the person in the creative-salvific project of God. To continue the mission of Jesus and to walk along with him in the horizon of the kingdom—even if many historical utopias have fallen—is an undeniable requirement of the gospel. But this will be possible only through an effective presence in the midst of the poor and the excluded. In fact, "the poor are those excluded from the system of the market, those who do not exist, those who are beyond the limits of the market. To affirm their existence, to hear their cry and to witness that God is in their midst is a way of denying the absoluteness of the market,"[15] and to question the character of the redeeming need of the sacrifice of human lives imposed by neoliberal theology. It is to support the resistance of the people, weakened and threatened in so many ways. This does not mean denying the market absolutely, but rather it means finding out how the market might correspond to the objective of a life of dignity for all, without exclusions, according to the design of God for humanity.

The second dimension is one of analysis and methodology. Mission today cannot exempt itself from the careful analysis of the globalized panorama of the contemporary world. It is a question of getting more adequate tools to strengthen the growth of a critical consciousness, civic and political, of persons, many of whom are deprived of their most elementary rights. As Pedro Ribeiro de Oliveira so aptly summarizes the situation:

> The system of the globalized market today was planned as structurally excluding . . . . Only a part of humanity has a place in the world's economic order: 80%?, 60%?, 40%?, or even less than that? No one can give an exact estimate of how many people will remain within the system and how many will be excluded from the system.[16]

An important or pertinent understanding of the concept and of the phenomenon of exclusion, in its specificity today, "when the masses of those excluded become 'surplus mass' . . . pariah or outcasts," without a function in a system which can perfectly well function without them, is essential under the risk of acting naively and placing mission at the service of the system. It does

---

[15] Jung Mo Sung, "Economía e idolatría: Desafios para la Iglesia en el siglo XXI," *Convergência* no. 33 (June 1997): 309.

[16] Pedro Ribeiro de Oliveira, "La Problemática subyacente al IX Encuentro Intereclesial de las CEB's," *Convergência* no. 33 (June 1997): 289.

not seem sensible not to profit from the social analytical moment under the pretext that the mediations are in crisis or are not pertinent.

The third dimension is that of practices and mediations. Here we find ourselves in the domain of the concrete, in the domain of the down-to-earth and functional. The growing awareness of exclusion as a worldwide and structural fact, of the specificity and the magnitude of the phenomenon of the excluded, makes it possible to articulate new practices and new mediations which permit us to advance in a more assured manner. Let us cite some of these practices, which are already being carried out in Latin America, at least in embryonic or incipient form:

- The courage to be countercultural, to go against the current, to admit and confess, against the pretensions of the main exponents of neoliberalism that "the social pit is not something fatal," as the French bishops affirmed in a recent document.

- A clear definition of the "place" that religious life and its institutions occupy in today's society, governed as it is by the laws of the neoliberal market, and of the type of mission it intends to be in that society. In this complex panorama "there is no possible neutrality: either the social forces— among which are the Christian churches and religious life— join with the system of the market, victor in the Cold War, or with the masses which this system excludes."[17] It is true that today the segment of religious life clearly choosing to follow this path in its mission is a minority. Nevertheless, in several countries we find concrete expressions of this option.

- Efforts to create partnerships among institutions, organizations, groups, and churches committed in the search for an alternative "project" (i.e., a fundamental re-visioning the common weal, society-as-a-whole) capable of overcoming the fatalistic absolutizing of the regnant "system"—as if it is beyond human possibilities to make a difference. In this sense, Pedro Ribeiro de Oliveira speaks about an inversion

---

[17] Ibid., 291.

of the terms of the problem, "rejecting the idea that integration into the market can solve the problem of poverty, this trend has its place in the periphery of the system and it assumes the perspective of the excluded in order to propose a political and economic paradigm subordinated to respect for the environment and for humanity, and an austere lifestyle of solidarity, looking toward the realization of an alternative world."[18] This is also the point of view adopted by the bishops of France in the aforementioned document: "It is necessary that we learn anew a certain common temperance in order to distribute the advantages of progress." Without regulations, progress alienates. The bishops of Brazil, for their part, insist on an evangelization "committed to bringing about a transformation in the country and the development of a civilization which, cultivating sobriety and sharing, will respect and value life, and the greatness and the limitations of nature."[19]

- Collaborating to bring about the birth and expansion of networks of solidarity. This is above all at the popular level and at the level of the nongovernmental organizations that place themselves at the service of the common good to further coresponsibility for the present and the future of the nation, overcome the ill-fated tendency to individualism and to competitiveness which the system fosters and nourishes, and reject the impoverishment of the people as an unavoidable cost for excluding economic development. The role in giving expression to and empowering these networks is clear. In great part, it is here where breaches are opened, small as they may be, for the organization and the resistance of the people.

- Maintaining presence and acting in international instances of political and economic power, where the lot of the people is decided in an authoritarian manner and where, in one way or another, the voice of solidarity, prophetic denunciation, and the cry for justice needs to be heard. Several orders and

---

[18] Ibid., 290.
[19] National Conference of Brazilian Bishops, "Vida con dignidade," 2.

international congregations, both male and female, have persons qualified for this difficult task, and they are beginning to be in those spaces which will no doubt constitute a truly new areopagus.

The Poor as Witnesses to the Kingdom

Lift up your eyes, and see how the fields are already white for harvest. . . . The Samaritans asked him to stay with them; and he stayed there two days. . . . They said to the woman . . . "We have heard for ourselves, and we know that this is indeed the Savior of the World." (John 4:36, 40-42)

The word of Jesus to his apostles at the well reminds disciples, men and women, of all times that there are always fields already white for the harvest. We have to know how to identify those fields and to discern the ways the Spirit opens before us for this divine harvest. Without trying to predict the future, or to fall into naïvely wanting to define complete new directions in mission, we can nonetheless indicate five of the conditions of this harvest to which the Spirit is leading us by means of, as it were, "new signs of the times."

1. A More Cosmic and Holistic Anthropology

Progress in science has shown the close interrelationship of the person to the cosmos and the need for a more integrated and integrating vision of things, better able to bring about unity, more holistic. This does not mean giving up the centrality of the person in God's plan, but rather becoming aware that "life, matter, and the spirit, the here and the beyond, are intimately interconnected. This makes possible the creation of a view of the world which will truly be all-encompassing, which embraces and includes globality, totality,"[20] as a basis for mission. That new anthropology will make possible a more integrated and open religious life, one with wider horizons, more in harmony with what is beauti-

---

[20] João Batista Libânio, "Diferentes paradigmas na história de Téologia," in *Teologia e novos paradigmas* (São Paulo: Loyola, 1996), 47.

ful, simple, human, joyful, cheerful, with nature, and with everything. It will be a religious life that will try to situate itself not in
the horizon of neoliberal global capitalism, but within the horizon of universal solidarity and the worldwide networking of
human relationships, in which there is no place for exclusion—
wherever one's origins may be—and in which relationships are
based on respect for the person, for nature, and for the cosmos,
where relationships are expressions of the values of the gospel
and the utopia of the kingdom.

2. Communion in Mission

Envisioned here is a communion in mission built precisely on
differences, plurality, and diversity, rather than in spite of them.
An intense experience of God as Trinity, of God as love and relationship, will give coherence and truth to that communion, making it possible to recreate it every day. Mission articulated from
this perspective will know how to relativize bureaucratic-institu-
tional and normative elements in favor of life and unity under the
guidance of the Spirit. Given how contemporary society is, the
sense and the necessity of such a witness to communion in mission are an enormous challenge, demanding a constant listening
to the Word, an evangelical boldness and humble disposition to
overcome differences and conflicts.

3. An Intense Experience of Diaspora in the World

Big institutions and grand works will become ever less the center for religious communities (both for individual provinces and
for congregations as wholes), nor will they serve as a basis for
mission. The reduced number of personnel and the option to situate themselves in the margins of power will gradually lead men
and women religious to ally themselves with men and women of
other faiths and cultures. They will be in solidarity with them,
and committed to building justice and peace, equality and love,
among the peoples and the nations. Religious life will make itself
heard in the new areopagoi, not because of grandiloquent
speeches or extensive institutions, but because of its presence in
dialogue, and its ability to engage in resistance. It will be heard
for its utter simplicity of faith and hope in situations of crisis, for

its capacity to be humble, yet vigorously prophetic and counter-cultural, in the way of the exodus and of *kenosis*.

Effectiveness in undertaking diverse tasks and engendering strong cohesion in the unique mission of Jesus (presumed by the whole community of the congregation because of its founding charism) will require more agility in decision making, more trust in persons and in their personal charisms, more boldness in running the risk of unity in dispersion and diaspora. All of this could lead to a corporate (not only personal) experience of *kenosis,* of being stripped bare, of humble acceptance of one's own vulnerability and contingency. But "if the grain of wheat does not fall to the ground and die . . . ."

4. The Kingdom as Horizon of Life and Mission

Only the commitment to the kingdom, with its demands for conversion, for truth, and for justice, justifies the radical options which the mission of religious life presupposes, and will continue to presuppose at the millennium's turn. From this perspective, mission will progressively lead religious life to new forms of option for the poor and the excluded. It will lead religious life to clear and creative collaboration with persons and institutions which have political, social, and cultural commitments that question and transform the status quo. It will lead religious life to an effective acknowledgment of the role of the laity in the mission of the church and of religious life, and to a declericalization of mission, ministries, and the ecclesial and religious community. In fact, religious communities (at both the provincial and congregational level) both now and in the future will either join the great trend toward solidarity that is coming about on the margins of society, or they will lose their strength and their savor as the salt of which Jesus speaks: they will cease to be prophetic signs of the kingdom.

5. Jesus and His Gospel

The goods news of the kingdom is the unique reason for our existence. This means that religious life must celebrate, in the Eucharist and in life, without dichotomizing the two or distorting them, the "subversive memory" of Jesus. It must confess, more with what it does than what it says, its faith in his person and in his cause—the kingdom—even when this implies the risk of having to surrender one's life. It must proclaim in the new areopagus, in the diaspora, in the center and at the periphery of the globalized world, the good news of the Master, creating anew in history his liberating practices and his absolute filial and deep fidelity to the God of the kingdom.

It is easy to realize that these new circumstances will hold greater possibilities of responding to challenges (and thus will hold out a future) to those communities which are indeed communities in mission—communities that are participatory and in dialogue, respectful of difference, critical toward ideologies and systems, able to make decisions with evangelical boldness and in truly spiritual-communitarian discernment; communities that are ready to share freely and in depth their life experiences and experiences of mission and faith, of being profoundly centered on the person and cause of Jesus. All of this presupposes a living awareness of the equality of all persons, the fostering of the evangelical value of mutual service. This creates and nourishes relationships of respect and acceptance of the plurality of cultures, races, beliefs, mentalities, opinions, and ways of being, recognizing them as gifts of the Spirit for the building up of the kingdom.

By Way of Conclusion

The first Council of the church of Jesus Christ took place in the year 49/50 in the city of Jerusalem. The great and most serious question under discussion was how to proclaim Jesus Christ and to live out his message in a non-Jewish world. Two possible ways of deciding this question were offered to the apostles. They could continue to be constituted as a Jewish sect, living within the boundaries of Jewish religious and cultural village life and of the Middle East. Or they could go beyond the frontiers of the Jewish world, opening themselves to new cultural and religious settings, adopting new symbols, reshaping concepts, refashioning their worship and rites, taking the risk of losing themselves. It was the price to be paid if they wanted to transform themselves from a Palestinian sect into a religion that was catholic and universal. In the face of that dilemma, the apostles, filled with the Holy Spirit, had the courage to choose the second way, refounding nascent Christianity completely.[21]

There are unmistakable signs that religious life today finds itself before a challenge similar to that of first-century Christianity: either it must radically rethink its structures of life and mission, or run the risk of domesticating the Spirit and paralyzing its life. In that new junction in which it finds itself, the parable of the Samaritan woman is paradigmatic. The missionary activity of Jesus is exocentric in relation to the systems, power, and customs of his time, and this in a twofold way. The center for Jesus is at the margins, and the marginalized and excluded are drawn by him to the center. In the parable of the Samaritan woman, the exocentric character of the mission of Jesus and of the kingdom he proclaims is evident. It causes perplexity and even scandal to the disciples. Barriers of religion and race crumble. The messianic revelation is extended like the noontime sun in a context and with interlocutors unthought of before. Led by the Spirit, the woman breaks her silence. Her word is the only bridge that connects back with the original Source. Mission acquires unsuspected dimensions. It becomes like an unstoppable river of living water. The kingdom becomes a historical truth in the lives of the little ones and those who are despised, the ones who accept the salvific-liberating word of Jesus.

Latin America is the golden field ready for the divine harvest, where the evil effects of an excluding system incorporate the figure of the non-kingdom. Great multitudes are being driven to the margins. Jesus is the model to be continuously recreated by the disciples, and the missionary "itinerancy" of the Master the paradigm of mission to be reassured with evangelical boldness and prophetic-liberating clarity. And that puts serious questions before us. What do we do as a community, as ecclesiastical institutions, to prevent the human community from being ever more enslaved by new forms of poverty and exclusion? Do we try to think of the world with the excluded as our starting point, in the certain knowledge that they are today the "criterion of judgment

---

[21] Prudente Nery, "Refundacão da vida religiosa," in *Vida Religiosa em face do Terceiro Melênio* (São Paulo: CRB/Loyola, 1997), 21-26.

of history"? Are we in fact—our persons, our institutions, and our practices—on the side of those who are excluded by reason of their class, race, color of skin, gender, or for any other reasons? When we make decisions, do we truly ask ourselves how our decisions affect the life of the poor and what impact they will have on the whole of society? Can we be counted among those who courageously struggle to live in a nonexcluding society? Is this not the time to open up pathways beyond strict evangelization and join with all those who defend the rights of the poor and the excluded, who respect the dignity of life, who struggle for greater justice, so as to promote solidarity and peace, who are careful to find viable alternatives for social life, beyond all possible ideological differences and religious creed?

Response to María Carmelita de Freitas, F.I.

Robert J. Schreiter, C.PP.S.

THROUGH MUCH OF THIS CONGRESS, OUR APPROACH TO THE future of mission has been through the lens of geography. We have moved from one geographic region of the world to the next and looked at issues facing mission from the perspective of different contexts. This is a useful and indeed an important way to approach mission, and it has proven very fruitful for our reflections. Sister María de Freitas's presentation provides us that angle of vision as well, but adds another important kind of reflection, namely, on the agents of mission—in this case, women and men religious who are engaged in mission. Most of the mission *ad gentes* carried out by the Roman Catholic Church in the world today is done through the agency of these religious, so it bears reflecting on just how they—or better, we—see our vocation and how we will respond to that call to mission.

Sister de Freitas helpfully moves back and forth among many of the factors that have influenced religious in mission worldwide, and the specific experiences of those coming from and working in Latin America. This twofold perspective is one that can be used by religious working anywhere in the world to reflect on their own situation as one of working in a concrete, local place, yet being part of a worldwide church. She first recalls the reception of the call of the Second Vatican Council to renew religious life by returning to the charism of the founding figures of religious institutes, in light of the reality in which religious found themselves working. She relates how the powerful convergence of the insights of the Second Vatican Council with the remarkable renaissance of the Latin American church, so eloquently reflected in the meetings of El Consejo Episcopal Latinoamericano (CELAM) in Medellín and Puebla, created such a stimulating vision of the call to religious life and to mission. Through the work of the Conference of Latin American Religious (CLAR), this vision was translated into what she calls the hermeneutical key of liberation, that is, the capacity to see the actual situation of Latin America from the perspective of the poor crying out to the God of life for their liberation. Through the *comunidades eclesiales de base*—the small Christian communities—through specific pastoral plans, through living a life immersed (*insertada*) in and identified with the realities of the poor, and through the theology of liberation, religious in Latin America developed one of the most creative and visionary inculturations of religious life and of mission to be found anywhere in the world. To put it in her own words:

> What does it mean to allow oneself to be evangelized by the poor? How do we evangelize from the perspective of the poor? How to live out justice and solidarity in a society that is structurally unjust? How can we accept the inevitable conflict coming to those who live in solidarity with the poor? How can we be agents of a holistic liberation? How can we break with and form a new relationship with the past?

Mission became the hermeneutical key to living out this new vision of religious life.

The second part of Sr. de Freitas's presentation takes us into the present situation, one characterized by economic globalization. It has created what she and many others have called a *neoliberal world*, that is, a brand of capitalism that is based on unregulated and unfettered markets, much like those of the liberal capitalism of the late nineteenth century. Drawing upon the work of many Latin American critics of neoliberal capitalism, she describes the dynamics of neoliberalism as a false religion. Like religion, it is all-encompassing and all-demanding of its followers. Its hidden god is the anonymous and unregulated financial forces which drive the relentess search for profit. For those who benefit from it, neoliberal capitalism offers immediate reward. For the poor who do not benefit, neoliberal capitalism offers an eschatology, promising benefits in some distant world to come. But the market represents the only reality: "outside the market there is no salvation"—*extra mercatum nulla salus*.

To what is the missionary called in such a situation of idolatry? The gods may be false, but they are not inert idols. They wreak profound misery upon the poor with their "structural adjustments" of the economy, forcing the poor into ever greater poverty. They create a logic of *exclusion*, which becomes the principal fact of our times. It is driven by a logic of efficiency and a cult of consumption. How is the missionary to respond to this exclusion? To her credit, Sr. de Freitas acknowledges that the rise of economic globalization represents a profound change of circumstances from those which gave rise to the creative synthesis of religious life and mission in the 1960s and 1970s. Not everyone has been able to see this. To be sure, the majority of the Latin American population was poor in that period, and they continue to be (although even more so) today. But how they are being made even poorer, and what will be necessary to liberate them from that poverty represent a different set of circumstances. This she recognizes. She presents what has been the response to date— what she calls a prophetic and countercultural resistance, typified as *solidarity*. But at the same time—and this is the third part of her presentation—she wonders just what form missionary witness by religious will need to take in this neoliberal world.

In that third part, she outlines the concrete forms solidarity will have to take in order to achieve that resistance. She calls too for a new analysis and the building of a new methodology to counter the false religion of neoliberal capitalism. What Sr. de Freitas has given us in this carefully reasoned analysis is a blueprint for what religious engaged in mission have to do everywhere in the world today. If Vatican II's teaching on religious life and mission spurred us into a renewal of both our fidelity to the charisms of our founders and foundresses and of our work in mission, today we face everywhere a false religion in neoliberal capitalism. What we have experienced and learned from the renewal that followed Vatican II will continue to be the platform from which we move into this new reality, as Sr. de Freitas clearly points out. Yet our response to this reality will have to be different. The resistance needed against neoliberal capitalism is different from the resistance to the national security state of the 1970s and early 1980s. A complicating factor too is that the hierarchical leadership of the church has moved to a different place. It has been withdrawing from engagement with the world. The effect of this withdrawal is a tacit endorsement of the status quo. The voices of Medellín and Puebla do not find their counterpart in this neoliberal world.

Sister de Freitas does not give us more than an outline of what needs to be done. In many ways, that may be more useful at this time than a detailed plan. It is an invitation to us all, each in our own location, to reflect on what kind of solidarity with the poor and excluded we are being called to. How shall mission take shape in this new kind of world? How will the resources developed in the latter half of the twentieth century for mission serve us now in this twenty-first century? In my own way, I hope to offer one response to these questions in the next presentation. Suffice it for now to say the following:

- We cannot simply repeat the formulae that have served us in the past. We must rather reflect on them in a way that allows us to draw forth from them what will help us most in this new situation.

- We must analyze the neoliberal situation and not simply remain content to denounce it. Denunciation may give us the comfort of feeling prophetic, but it may not in itself really change much in such an all-pervasive reality.

- We must continue to address ourselves to the God of life. We must enter yet again into the paschal mystery of the Lord's suffering and death. Resurrection always comes as a somewhat unimagined thing. So will no doubt be the outcome of our missionary witness in the face of globalization.

Sister de Freitas has given us a stimulating and well-thought-out presentation. It was not only a good analysis of where we have been and where we now find ourselves. It also proposed a missionary spirituality. She uses to great effect the story of Jesus' encounter with the Samaritan woman at the well from John 4. A new missionary vision for the twenty-first century will need a spirituality to accompany and sustain it. In John 4 we may well have the seeds for such a spirituality, much as the powerful images of the exodus and the Emmaus story shaped the postconciliar missionary effort for so many of us.

6

Globalization and Reconciliation

Challenges to Mission

Robert J. Schreiter, C.PP.S.

Mission in a New Century

THE CELEBRATION OF A JUBILEE YEAR GIVES US THE OPPOR-
tunity to review our past, acknowledge our failings, and seek forgiveness for our sins. It also allows us to renew our commitment
to Christ and to the reign of God which he is bringing about. For
this reason, it is an especially appropriate time to look at our participation in the church's mission and to reorient our direction in
that mission as needed. That, in fact, has been the purpose of this
special missionary congress. For mission to be truly faithful to the
Lord's directive, and to be truly effective in the world to which it
is addressed, such periodic reflections are necessary. The wealth
of insight and spirituality we can draw from the Scriptures and
the church's tradition are such that not all elements can be
focused upon at the same time: we must choose the most appropriate and compelling point of reference by which to orient our
work in mission. Likewise, the world in which mission is carried
out continues to change and develop. The Word which that world
needs to hear, therefore, must be chosen so that through it the
world might come to hear the fullness of God's message in Jesus
Christ. The Jubilee is an opportunity to stop to make that

reassessment, so as to strengthen the quality of our witness to what God has done for the world in Jesus Christ.

I think that the reflection to which we are called in this Jubilee Year 2000 is particularly apposite. The principal reason is not the ending of one millennium of Christianity and the beginning of another. Important as that might be in marking the milestones along the way to the realization of God's reign, calendars remain, after all, rather arbitrary milestones in the life and events of the world. More important, it seems to me, is the fact that we are now some ten years into the making of a new world order, a new configuration of the relationships that shape the political, economic, and social order of our world. The British historian Eric Hobsbawm has dubbed the twentieth century "the short century." According to his reckoning, it extended from 1914, when the great powers of Europe went to war and began the breakdown of the world order of the nineteenth century, to 1989, when the world order that grew out of the destruction of two World Wars itself came to an end with the breaching of the Berlin Wall. The bipolar world of democratic and communist societies, of capitalism and socialism, effectively ended in that symbolic event. The 1990s, the decade of our immediate past, was the period in which the world has been largely in turmoil. I do not think we are at the end of that transition process to a new world order. Nonetheless, after a decade of experience, some things do seem to be coming into clearer view. Collectively, those things come best under the rubric of globalization. Globalization appears to be the best frame by which we can interpret and engage the world in response to our call to participate in the bringing about of the Reign of God in our world. The first part of this presentation, then, will deal with trying to understand what globalization is as a form of world order, and what challenges it portends for the conduct of mission in the years ahead.

To look at the world into which we are sent is, of course, only one part of what fidelity to the mission of Christ and the church in the world means for us. We must examine our own reading and living out of the tradition that has been handed down to us in the Scriptures, the church's tradition, and the reflection on those riches by those who have gone before us. These provide us with the resources both to gauge our fidelity to the mission that we undertake, and the spirituality to sustain us in that mission.

Bringing out from that storehouse of Scripture and the tradition that builds upon it—the old as well as the new, as it were (Matt. 13:52)—we hope to renew our motivation and our capacity to engage in mission.

Mission institutes have renewed their sense of mission with the teachings of the Second Vatican Council and the subsequent magisterial teachings of the pope and the bishops, and their own reflections in such settings as the 1981 SEDOS Seminar on Mission. The impetus to that sense of renewal of mission came from the council and its call to renewal and reform, especially as it affected our sense of the church, the church's relation to the world, mission, and the role of religious institutes within it. At the same time, the development of a new world order in the 1950s and 1960s, shaped largely by the end of colonial empires and the onset of the Cold War, caused its own challenge to understanding how mission should be undertaken.

It will be important to reflect on the missionary theology and spirituality that have developed since the Vatican Council for two reasons. First of all, it has become for mission institutes a powerful resource for their own identities. It is also the basis for any subsequent change in our understanding of what mission for us means in our time. This theology and spirituality have been expressed in a variety of ways in all their richness in the course of this congress.

A second reason for reflecting on this heritage and resource is that it is the predominant way of approaching mission by religious institutes. I daresay that all of us here have been deeply formed by the postconciliar understanding of mission and the spirituality needed to sustain that mission. It is wrapped up in the very renewal of our understanding of the charism of our founders and foundresses, and how we read the signs of our own times. However, to the extent that this reading of the basis for mission is linked with a world order that has, in large part, departed from the world's stage, to that extent we must be open to a new vision to analyze the signs of our times and to shape spiritually what we do by way of mission in our world. I say "to the extent" advisedly. The world has not changed utterly and completely since 1989. But enough changes have taken place, and enough trends have consolidated themselves, to make such a new look incumbent upon us. I think that, for a group such as SEDOS, this is especially important, since you constitute the leadership at the general level of your missionary institutes. You are in a position to have a wider vision which many of your members, working hard at the grass-roots level, may not have yet surely need. If the leadership at the general level cannot think past the paradigms that have been formative for them in order to see a different kind of world coming about, then it is failing in its responsibility.

The second part of this presentation will focus on missionary theology and spirituality, suggesting what might be the outline of such a theology and spirituality to meet the changes we have been experiencing in the world order. I will propose reconciliation as a model for mission.

A final note before beginning: Following the schema for this congress, I will be addressing the questions of world order and missionary response from the perspective of North America, specifically the United States. I do this, first of all, because that is where I come from and where I live. Although I have struggled to learn from other parts of the world, it would be naïve to think that my location and perspective can be so easily changed. What I say must be received with this background in mind, even as I try to represent a broader perspective. Second, given the power exercised by the United States in the world today—economically, militarily, politically, and culturally—the impact of the United States on world order and missionary response has to be addressed squarely.

At the same time, no engagement with the world and with the mission of Christ is unalloyed good or irredeemably evil on our part. My hope is to express some of the positive contributions that insights and actions on behalf of mission from North America might offer, in spite of the negative experience that much of what comes out of that region of the world may be for so many in mission.

Globalization as the Context for Mission Today

Let us turn then to the context of mission today, the world order as it is taking shape. As was mentioned above, I do not believe that we have settled into a world order of the clear type that the colonial empires of the nineteenth century or the Cold

War of the last half of the twentieth century provided. However, the contours of a world order are discernible in the current situation, and it is upon these that I would like to draw.

"Globalization" is the generic term in English (*mondialisation* is preferred in French and some other languages) for the world order that appears to be taking shape. Globalization as a phenomenon revolves around two axes. The first axis is *connectedness*. Advances in communications technologies in the last quarter of the twentieth century made possible the development of a communications network that allows people and institutions to be in contact with one another at a level and at a pace that was unthinkable before that time. The symbol for this connectedness, which emerged in the 1990s, is the Internet and the World Wide Web. The prospects held out by the interconnectedness are indeed nearly overwhelming. The interconnections already possible make the flow of information quick and easy to access. They also democratize communication dramatically, cutting through hierarchies that earlier could control the flow of information. Through other media the sense of interconnectedness can likewise be enhanced. One need only think of how the world celebrations of the turn of the millennium were broadcast on television on New Year's day of 2000.

But interconnectedness has its downside as well. This is *exclusion*, a theme that has been reflected upon by those who not only do not benefit from globalization, but who are disadvantaged and oppressed by it. The interconnectedness has its conditions and limitations. At the level of communication, it requires access to a telephone. For Europeans and North Americans, where there is a telephone now available at the rate of seven hundred telephones per every thousand people, the fulfillment of the promises awaits. In Chad or Bangladesh, where there are only two telephones per thousand people, the promises are empty ones. The economic flows that globalization promotes lead to greater concentrations of wealth in those who have access and resources already. For those who do not, they not only do not improve in their lot, but they actually get worse. Although no one has been able to measure this exactly, the general estimate is that approximately 20 percent of the world's population benefits from globalization, while 80 percent find their position worsened. If the poor had become central to an understanding of mission during the Cold War period, their situation cries out even more for action today.

The second axis around which globalization revolves is an understanding of *space*. Time was the organizing element of much of the modern age and the societies that went with it. Empire was justified by Europe on the basis that the peoples they encountered on their adventures were "primitive," that is, came from an earlier time and needed to "catch up" with the "advanced" world. The development of evolutionary thinking in the nineteenth century provided "time-lines" along which to organize an understanding of the diversity of the world.[1] Industry sought forms of efficiency (Taylorism) that would speed up production and so cut costs.

In a globalized world, time means increasingly little, since communication can be nearly instantaneous to any part of the world, thanks to the Internet. Time in an existential sense continues to exist, of course. But globalized societies tend to imitate this instantaneity of time, by trying to push more and more events into ever smaller time frames. In a way, time becomes now the worthless possession of the poor, who have plenty of time and are made to wait in welfare office lines, in waiting rooms for health care, and of the elderly, who wait to die because they are no longer useful in a globalized economy.

Space is expressed in two dimensions. On the one hand, it has become incredibly compressed. When one thinks how much information can be put on a single microchip, it is nothing short of amazing. The social counterpart of the microchips in our computers is the global city. There are now more than four hundred cities in the world that have a population of more than a million inhabitants. Mexico City has more inhabitants than the vast continent of Australia. Here human beings are compressed into spaces that cannot sustain them at any level of humanness.

On the other hand, the compression of space, combined with the instantaneous nature of communication, means that space is deterritorialized. This is most evident in the flow of communication and the distribution of wealth in the world today. Once one

---

[1] On this matter, see Johannes Fabian, *Time and the Other* (New York: Columbia University Press, 1987).

could chart the world as one of center and periphery, with Europe as the center of empire, and its colonies on the periphery. Today, the world map cannot be drawn so easily. The wealthy elites in poor countries may identify more with one another than with the disadvantaged denizens of their own country. Citizenship and communal responsibility are eroded. One gets the phenomenon known as "Brazilianization," where enclaves of the rich live in relative detachment from the poor who are right along side them territorially.

Moreover, this deterritorialization of the world makes dichotomous thinking about the world less useful in analysis, since boundaries are not drawn as sharply. For example, even to speak of exclusion as a category is somewhat inaccurate. To be sure, the poor are excluded from the benefits of a globalized world. But they are not excluded from bombardment by the media with the cultural icons of globalization, nor are their forms of employment excluded from the powerful streams of the neoliberal economy. The world becomes polycentric rather than bipolar, more like a pattern of turbulence than push-and-pull, more a field of contention than a battle line between center and periphery.[2]

To get a clearer picture of globalization, one can sketch its effects briefly by looking at four dimensions of human life that are being changed by it: communications, economics, politics, and the sociocultural sphere.

Communications

Something of globalization's impact on communications has already been sketched above. The capacity for communications, which allows for moving large amounts of information rapidly, is at the heart of the globalization process. Communications technology lies at the basis of the transformation of finances and the democratization of access to information. It also allows people to network independently of the hierarchical patterns that heretofore could block such communications flow. Thus the network of support that led to most countries of the world signing a treaty

---

[2] For a discussion of these ways of looking at relations within a globalized world, see Nikos Papastergiadis, *The Turbulence of Migration* (London: Routledge, 2000).

banning land mines did not come out of government leaders in summit meetings or the efforts of parliaments; the campaign was put together completely on the Internet. The value of interconnectedness is also much in evidence in the world of science, where it allows researchers in different parts of the world to collaborate together on research projects.

By the same token, those who are not part of these communications networks do not benefit from what this greater interconnectedness may offer, even as their worlds are invaded by media. Issues of human solidarity are prominent here.

Economics

Globalization is most in evidence in the economic sphere. The collapse of state socialism has left the field wide open for the spread of capitalist economy. There are, to be sure, many different kinds of capitalism in the world today; it would be wrong to speak as though there were but a single type. The free-wheeling capitalism of the United States is not the same as the government-directed form of Japan and the social democratic forms favored in much of the European Union. The nascent capitalisms of Eastern Europe are yet another. However, they all communicate and connect with one another, and the United States takes a powerful leadership position.

Taken together, these capitalisms have come to be labeled "neoliberal," since they are reminiscent of the industrial capitalism of the late nineteenth century. They resist government control, try to escape regulation of any type, and seek to subordinate their responsibilities to the work force to the exigencies of competition and profit. Because of the reach and the power they derive from utilizing the available communications systems, they create the impression that there is no alternative to them—nor can there be any. A number of critics, such as Franz Hinkelammert, Jung Mo Sung, and Inázio Neutzling in Latin America, have noted how these totalizing tendencies of capitalism make it present itself as a kind of religion. That the market is absolute, that competition is the only possible action, and that profit is the ultimate value are transcendental claims meant to reconfigure the world for the sake of those who want to make money.

Neoliberal capitalism has enriched some, but it has impoverished many and made them more miserable. It is the claims and the consequences of neoliberal capitalism that have put forward the ugly face of globalization.

Politics

The fall of the Berlin Wall symbolized the end of Communism and the kind of socialism it proposed throughout much of the world. Many feel that its total demise is just a matter of time. Democracy was to have taken Communism's place in Eastern Europe and elsewhere, and that is slowly taking place in many countries. Democracy, however, rests on suppositions about civil society. Communism had tried to eradicate those elements of civil society, and these are not easily or quickly rebuilt. In some of the formerly Communist countries, criminal gangs and plutocratic thugs constitute the actual rule of the country.

Globalization's effects have three immediate consequences for the missionary activity that is our subject here. First of all, it has weakened the power of the nation-state. Transnational corporations can run roughshod over governments' attempts to regulate them. While the state has been weakened, it will not disappear, since there are still functions for it that even neoliberal capitalism depends on. Ironically, neoliberal capitalism also strengthens the state in some ways. Countries now need central banks to deal with investors and the International Monetary Fund.[3] The weakening of the nation-state also raises questions about world governance. The emergence of trade organizations poses the possibility of new forms of governance. The United Nations finds itself in a period of scrutiny about what its future direction might be, and the proliferation of non-governmental organizations (NGOs) offers new horizons in cooperation and human promotion.

Second, the weakening of the nation-state—either by transnational capitalism or by the lack of the structures to support

---

[3] This whole area is being studied especially by Saskia Sassen; see, e.g., her *Losing Control? Sovereignty in an Age of Globalization* (New York: Columbia University Press, 1996).

democracy—has laid open the possibility of ethnic groups arising within nation-states and claiming autonomy. War is more likely now to be waged within states between groups rather than between nations. War itself is changing, through a combination of new technology and new politics. The United States of America, by far the strongest military power in the world, was unable to impose its will in Iraq, Somalia, or the Balkans during the 1990s. At the same time, localized wars have devastated states in Africa and central Asia.

Third, the fact that there is no alternative on the horizon to neoliberal capitalism at this time has meant at least a temporary suspension of utopian thinking. The capacity to imagine and to work toward an alternative form of economics and politics stirred strong waves of hope among missionaries and among sectors of the poor in the 1960s and 1970s, a time when many of you were formed spiritually and intellectually for missionary work. The "third way" of some European democrats has yet to constitute a real alternative; it looks more like trying to make the harsher demands of neoliberalism more palatable. While not wanting simply to acquiesce to neoliberal capitalism, it is also foolhardy to expect that it will disappear any time soon. It seems best to engage in two forms of activity: (1) to work at building or rebuilding the intermediate structures of society that can engage the macrostructures more effectively; and (2) to support the kind of work that NGOs have been able to do in the areas of ecology, political change, building of mass opinion, and networking of otherwise isolated groups.

Sociocultural Sphere

Three things need to be noted about how globalization has changed the sociocultural sphere. The first is migration. The globalization of the economy and the relative ease of long-distance travel have drawn (and forced) large segments of the population into migration in search of economic betterment. What has become most striking in recent years is that a majority of these migrants are women—and a not insignificant number are children. All of these migrants work in low-paying jobs and have no protection of their rights. Add to the migrants the more than one hundred million refugees from political violence, and one has genuine social turbulence in the world. They are recreating the urban agglomerations of the world in a way that is only beginning to be studied.

Second, the circulation of icons of culture, emanating especially from the United States, has transformed the desires and the self-images of people around the world, especially the youth, who make up the great majority of the population in many poor countries. The clothing, food, and entertainment propagated in the media define what belonging to this world "community" means, and the image of the human held up to the youth is that of being a consumer. Production and consumption of goods become the defining points of being human in this globalized world. The old who can no longer produce, the poor who do not have the means either to produce or to consume are written off and excluded from the juggernaut of globalization.

Third, the powerful reaction and resentment that the effects of globalization stir up in those who are excluded in one way or another make them turn to means of resistance. The claims of ethnicity may draw on ancient wrongs remembered, but many ethnic claims are attempts to stake out identity and a measure of power. Attempts at developing multicultural societies run the risk of running aground when conflict causes people to revert to old patterns and attitudes. Thus, many second-generation immigrants in France from the Maghreb (rim of northern Africa) reasserted Arab identity when Islam was vilified during the Gulf War.[4] Not only cultural identity but also religion becomes a resource of resistance and is revitalized in a variety of fundamentalisms. The relation of religion and violence is becoming a central theme that needs closer attention in our world today, but it cannot be explored further at this point.[5]

This may have seemed a long excursus on globalization, even though it could not do justice to the amount of work being done on the topic. What I hope I have made clear is, first of all, that globalization has already so woven itself into the fabric of the

---

[4] See, e.g., the work of Michel Wieviorka and others in *La France raciste* (Paris: Seuil, 1992).

[5] See, e.g., R. Scott Appleby, *The Ambivalence of the Sacred* (London: Rowman & Littlefield, 2000); and Mark Juergensmeyer, *Terror in the Mind of God* (Berkeley: University of California Press, 2000).

world that it is not likely—as an economic, political, and socio-cultural phenomenon—to disappear quickly. It has greater staying power than the ideology of the national security state, which is built largely on military power and maintaining social privilege, and was so formative to the early stages of Latin American liberation theologies. My guess is that it will last as least as long as the other great ideologies and social arrangements of modernity—a half century or more. As a result, we must see ways of analysis that will engage it critically, rather than trying to ignore it or subject it to our familiar ways of thinking.

Second, we must seek ways of engaging globalization, so that we do not engage in ineffective resistance, succumb to its enticements, or resign ourselves to inevitability. Here we need not only astute analysis but also engagement.

To illustrate these two points, let me give one example of analysis and one of engagement to illustrate what we might undertake in the new millennium to engage globalization for the sake of mission. The example of analysis has to do with whether globalization is simply the latest form of colonialism, and therefore should be treated accordingly. The engagement has to do with utilizing communication as international religious institutes to reshape globalization's agenda.

Is Globalization a New Colonialism?

A superficial analysis of the capitalisms at work in the contemporary global arena would lead one to believe that globalization represents the latest colonial and imperial venture of Europe and North America in our world. There are theorists of globalization themselves, such as Immanuel Wallerstein, who make this the backbone of their own presentation. After all, it would appear that many of the effects of globalization are the same as those of colonialism: peoples are robbed of their sovereignty; they lose control over their natural resources; their ways of life are disrupted by cultural requirements laid upon them from outside; and their lives are dictated by distant centers of power. The ideals held up to them of the human are unattainable and serve only to make them feel inferior.

On the surface, the parallels appear to be true. In the wake of globalization, the lives of those affected may be little different from what life was under colonializers two or three generations ago. From the side of the receivers, therefore, it makes little difference whether you call it globalization or colonialism; the effects are all the same. But if one wants to work through to break the effects of globalization on a people, the tools used to resist colonialism may turn out to be the wrong instruments. Globalization as a form of world order is constituted differently. Imperialism or colonial empire had a strong political base of a state-centered control. It had economic goals, but was directed by a political power that could be identified. It was strongly territorial in nature, both in who was colonized and who was the colonizer. Boundaries between colonized and colonizer were kept clear.[6]

As we have seen above, the political does not take the lead in the globalization process, but is struggling itself to keep up. It does not have an identifiable center. The United States is pointed to as the leading culprit, which in a way it is. But there is no identifiable center within the United States which, if confronted, could change the direction of globalization by itself. One might press the International Monetary Fund in this regard, but it now has an Australian director. The polycentric nature of globalization makes it hard to transform into the kind of enemy that responds to focused resistance. Contemporary global capitalism is not hierarchically organized like an empire. The deterritorialized nature of globalization, also discussed above, makes it hard to marshal poor countries against rich countries, since the wealthy of one country may identify more with their wealthy counterparts in other lands than with their own people. The peso crisis in Mexico in 1994 might be an example.

So what to do? New modes of resistance and survival must be sought. Utopias are designed in reaction to what can be seen and what causes suffering in the present. Alternatives must be built on the realities that we now experience; our horizons only stretch so far. A missionary task in this new millennium is to work on developing modes of analysis which address the situations that have

---

6 Helpful here is the work of Jan Nederveen Pieterse; see his "Globalization North and South: Representations of Uneven Development and the Interaction of Modernities," *Theory, Culture and Society* 17, no. 1 (2000): 129-37.

changed in our world and to present them in ways that are intelligible to our own membership and to those with whom they work. They must build too upon the strengths that have been developed in missionary engagement since the Vatican Council: our commitments to solidarity, especially with the poor; to accompaniment; to dialogue and inculturation; and to a God of life who wills liberation and well-being in the face of so much death.

Engagement: Communication

In order to engage globalization in a way that is critical and effective, we must build upon the analysis of globalization that we have undertaken. Fundamental to that is addressing the means of communication. It is communications technology that has made possible globalization as we have come to know it. Let me suggest two ways in which missionary institutes might do this.

First, we need to establish through communications media networks of solidarity. Earlier I mentioned how the enactment of the treaty banning land mines was developed mainly through networking on the Internet. This new type of political action represents a sophisticated way of understanding how the means of social communication work in a globalized world. Similar efforts at networking, on a smaller scale, have affected corporations in the area of ecology. The work that has been done in recent years by religious groups regarding global debt for poor countries again shows what the potential is here for action. In another arena, it is sometimes missionaries who become the only reliable source of information in situations of civil conflict. Because religious leaders may be the only ones who enjoy trust from different sides in a dispute, and the expatriate missionary may be the only one with reliable access to those beyond the conflict, those networks can become important sources for changing governmental and other opinion. In this regard, I think of the Africa Justice and Faith Network, based in Washington, D.C., and its efforts to influence U.S. political opinion regarding Africa.

Second, working with and creating nongovernmental organizations. NGOs have the capacity to play an ever larger role in the world, especially in the areas of peace-making, ecology, and the reconstruction of shattered societies. Much of the grass-roots and mid-range work at conflict resolution in the world today is being done by NGOs and workers in relief agencies, since wars affect civilian populations much more directly than was often the case in times past. Organizations such as Caritas are now called upon to help with civil reconstruction of societies along with providing more traditional relief services.

Missionary institutes within the church, and the Roman Catholic Church itself, are already constituted as international networks with their own channels of communication and their own access to centers of power in this polycentric world. In earlier generations, missionaries saved cultures by writing dictionaries and grammars of languages in oral cultures. Today their access to international networks of communication may hold back the hand of local governments or transnational corporations. There are examples already of religious institutes that have taken steps to organize NGOs accredited to the United Nations. The Franciscans and the Sisters of Mercy come to mind. This level of organization reflects the world in which we now live, where the global and the local intersect in so many different ways.

Let me conclude this section by emphasizing again what I think we need to address in looking toward how we might carry out mission faithfully and critically in the coming years. We must be aware of our context, and how globalization is shaping that context nearly everywhere. We must develop ways of examining not only the effects of globalization but what drives it and how it might be engaged. We must work to put in place the structures that will allow that engagement with a globalized world to be sustained and effective. Finally, we must prepare ourselves and our new members to be able to think in this way, much as we had to in the years after the Second Vatican Council.

Reconciliation as a Model for Mission

This brings us to the second part of this presentation. It is one thing to analyze and interpret the world in a way that we might engage it more directly for the sake of the coming of the reign of God. This attention to the context—and how the context has changed within our own lifetime—is a prerequisite for faithful and effective mission, but does not guarantee it. With this view of the world in which we live and act must go a reflection on just what it is we bring to this world. That is to say, just what is the good news of Jesus Christ for our time? The preparatory years for the Great Jubilee, mapped out first in Pope John Paul's *Tertio Millennio Adveniente*, have given us ample opportunity to reflect on our past and the heritage we have in the Scriptures and in the church. Where now might we find ourselves? Just what do we offer in this new millennium?

To begin this reflection, it might be helpful to recall where consideration of the teachings of the Vatican Council and the subsequent expressions of church teaching by popes, synods, and episcopal conferences, as well as efforts by SEDOS and religious institutes, has brought us. In the presentations that have been given in the course of this congress, we have heard that rich heritage reprised from the perspectives of different continents and different experiences of mission. North America has, on the whole, not made as lasting a contribution to this body of knowledge and spirituality as have other parts of the world, such as Latin America. One might aver that we have contributed more to the problem than to the solution! Yet to identify the missionary effort coming out of North America with the admittedly damaging elements of U.S. culture, or even the work of Protestant Pentecostal and fundamentalist missionaries, would be to sweep aside the work of so many North American missionaries who have struggled to be faithful and prophetic in their missionary activity.

If I were to look for words that capture the theology and spirituality of Catholic missionaries since the Second Vatican Council, they would be *incarnation, accompaniment,* and *solidarity.* The model of incarnation, of God sending his only Son into the world to be like us in all things but sin, has been at the heart of the renewed missionary vision. A theology and spirituality of an earlier period, which stressed the heroism and even the martyrdom of the missionary who risked his or her life to bring light into the darkness, to save souls, have been gradually replaced by a different spirituality since the middle of the twentieth century. That older vision, which inspired so many men and women to embrace a missionary vocation, was a theology and spirituality that partook deeply of the waters of the tradition and had made its own form of engagement with and response to the colonial adventures of Europe. It often borrowed the military metaphors of engaging in combat, winning territory, and planting European Christianity on foreign soil. At the same time, it could bring forth in missionaries a love for the people among whom they came, and it prompted them to resistance to the very colonial powers with whom they came. My purpose here is neither to analyze nor to judge this earlier time. It is only to sketch it in this rough fashion as itself a product of engagement with its context, so as to throw into greater relief the period immediately preceding our own.

The sense of distance in the earlier theology—between church and world, between religious and lay, between Europe and its colonies—was negated in the theology of the council for the sake of closer engagement. A theology of incarnation had helped prepare the way for this new understanding of mission. The Word entering the world better typified this understanding of missionary engagement. It was this theology of the incarnation that was evident in the council documents and laid the groundwork for the theology of inculturation that began to appear in the 1970s.

Accompaniment, a term first formulated in Latin American thought after the council, remains to my mind the best way of speaking about the theology of mission which followed the council. In Spanish, *acompanimiento* has much greater resonance than does its counterpart in English. It means not only walking alongside (rather than ahead) of someone; it bespeaks a constant being present to, and engaging with, the other. It was this walking alongside that has characterized postconciliar forms of mission. Rather than seeing themselves as superior to those among whom they worked, missionaries sought as much as possible to share and be with those whom they served. When the 1981 SEDOS Mission Seminar sought to define the forms of mission that had been emerging since the council, they identified four: proclamation, dialogue, inculturation, and liberation. Proclamation was to a great extent a continuation of the previous period of mission and an enduring aspect of all mission at any time. But dialogue, inculturation, and liberation constituted new avenues of being in mission, avenues that marked the road of accompaniment. The image of Jesus on the road to Emmaus with the disciples in Luke

24, and the charge in the scroll of Isaiah which Jesus reads in the synagogue in Nazareth in Luke 4, provided powerful images for this sense of missionary theology and spirituality.

Solidarity is a term first articulated in European trade unions in the nineteenth century. Since the late 1970s, it has become part and parcel of Catholic parlance, including at the level of papal teaching. Solidarity is the consequence of accompaniment, of living a life of dialogue, of inserting oneself into another's reality and struggling with others for the sake of liberation. It becomes an important way of representing the language of *communio* in the world in which we live.

Why might there be a need to articulate a new theology and spirituality of mission, given the power and the fruitfulness of incarnation, accompaniment, and solidarity as guideposts in a missionary vision? I do not believe that any of these has been superseded. They will endure as part of the missionary vision, just as proclamation endures. Yet, to go back to the beginning point of this presentation, the context in which these three elements of missionary theology and spirituality came to the fore has changed. A refocus may be needed. Here are some aspects of the changed context that may point to a need for a rethinking:

- Inculturation finds itself caught between official resistance from central church authority, on the one hand, and the ideological use of ethnicity in the local church, on the other.

- Theologies of liberation are caught between similar resistance and changed economic and political circumstances.

- No alternatives to global capitalism can be pointed to.

- Local communal violence threatens the prospects of interreligious dialogue.

- Resistance to oppression creates one kind of solidarity, but what kind of solidarity can be found in the slow and difficult process of social reconstruction?

Why Reconciliation Now?

The 1990s saw a dramatic increase of interest in reconciliation, which coincided with several important events:

- The end of communism in Eastern European countries, the end of military dictatorships and civil wars in Latin America, as well as the end of apartheid in South Africa all point to the need for the moral reconstruction of society.

- The celebration of the United Nations Year of the Indigenous in 1992 calls for colonial invaders to come to terms with their past treatment of native peoples.

- The discovery of the extent of domestic and sexual violence in families and within the church.

- The Jubilee Year as a time to seek forgiveness for the past and to enter more deeply into conversion.

All of these occurrences during the 1990s, with the interest in the Jubilee Year culminating in the pope's dramatic appeals for forgiveness during Lent of 2000, open up reconciliation as a new theme which might provide coherence to mission in a time of globalization.

Reconciliation is not in itself a univocal concept, nor are the motivations of those who invoke it universally shared. It received a strong ideological taint in Latin America in the 1980s when it was proposed as an alternative to liberation by the authors of the Los Andes statement. It has aroused nearly universal suspicion when former perpetrators of misdeeds call upon others to forget the past and to get on with the work of building the future. For some, reconciliation means conflict mediation. For others, it is about seeking justice for victims. For still others, it is coming to terms with the painful memories of the past. And for yet others, it is about the moral reconstruction of shattered societies.

Reconciliation is about all of these things—making peace, seeking justice, healing memories, rebuilding societies. At different stages of a society's journey, any and all of these may be called upon. It would not be possible to go into all of these here, nor to spell out completely what the implications would be for society or for missionary institutes.[7] However, it is possible to describe in

---

[7] I have tried to do this elsewhere in *Reconciliation: Mission and Ministry in a Changing Social Order* (Maryknoll, N.Y.: Orbis, 1992); *The Ministry of Reconciliation: Spirituality and Strategies* (Maryknoll, N.Y.: Orbis, 1998); "Mis-

broad lines why interest has become so great and what the Christian understanding of reconciliation might contribute, via the church's mission, toward a betterment of the world and a drawing closer to God's reign.

The cry for reconciliation grows out of an acute sense of the brokenness experienced on such a broad scale in the world today. It arises as people try to rebuild their lives in the ruins of ideological projects, civil conflict, the consequences of human malice and greed. It breaches the darkness of memory recovered from a painful past and the loss which that memory evokes. It is a calling out for a new set of relationships so that the terrible deeds done in the past cannot happen again—*nunca más*. It is a reaching out across the abyss of severed relationships to create a different kind of future for ourselves and especially for our children.

The language of reconciliation is on the lips of many people today. Christians bring their own reading of reconciliation to this, a reading that bears seeds of life for others as well. Christian understanding of reconciliation is rooted in the belief that reconciliation begins with the work of God in our lives, a work that has been made manifest to us in the life, death, and resurrection of Jesus Christ. Through Christ, God continues to effect reconciliation in our world.

Reconciliation is first and foremost the work of God in our lives. The enormity of the misdeeds of the past is so great that it overwhelms the human imagination to consider how they might ever be overcome. Who can undo the consequences of a war or of centuries of oppression? Who can bring back the dead? Who can restore a human life twisted by torture, mired in suffering, or stunted in its growth by loss and deprivation? Yet Christian faith in a God of life, a God of infinite care and mercy is at the base of the possibility of reconciliation. Yes, forgiveness can happen, but it is God who initiates it. A new possibility of life can be given to those who have suffered, but ultimately no wrongdoer can give that back; it will have to come from the Source of all life.

---

sion as a Model of Reconciliation," *Neue Zeitschrift für Missionswissenschaft* 52 (1996): 243-50; and "Reconciliation as Good News in a Divided World?" in *Las Americas se apren al nuevo milenio,* ed. Philippa Woodbridge and Carlos Pape (Rome: SEDOS, 1998), 210-23.

God is the one who initiates healing and restoration in the victim, and it is with the victim that God begins. Reconciliation does not depend ultimately on the repentance of the wrongdoer, because all too often the wrongdoer does not repent. To make reconciliation dependent on such a wrongdoer is to hold the victim hostage to the past and make the victim suffer once again. God heals and restores the dignity of the victim, taking the victim to a new place, making the victim a "new creation" (2 Cor 5:17). The victim is not restored to a *status quo ante*, but is brought to a new place from which the victim can come to see the world and its brokenness from God's own perspective, as it were, that is, from a perspective of grace and mercy. From there the victim can lead the wrongdoer to repentance—that is, not only to abjuring the deeds of the past but also to a new relation with the victim and the wrongdoer him- or herself.

Reconciliation seen from this perspective is about the possibility of a new creation. It is sanguine about how much and how often this is achieved in any fullness short of the coming of God's reign. But it does believe that a new future is possible. Belief in the resurrection of the dead stands as the horizon for this belief—namely, that even the dead shall experience justice.

The Ministry of Reconciliation

Christians are called to work toward this reconciliation—fully realizing all the time that it is ultimately the work of God, of whom they are but ambassadors (2 Cor. 5:19)—in at least two ways. First, they create *communities of reconciliation*, safe places where victims can come. There in an experience of safety they rebuild trust and prepare themselves to receive God's grace of reconciliation and empowerment. From this experience they can tread the difficult path to forgiveness and reconnecting their lives and their relationships.

Our religious institutes and the entire church are called in a special way in our time to be communities of reconciliation, those special spaces where God's saving action might break into people's lives. In order to be so, our institutes and our church must be places where the truth is spoken and lived, where domination and subjugation do not occur. This is the good news that a broken world yearns to hear.

Second, Christians must engage in the *moral reconstruction of broken societies*. This activity takes place on a variety of levels. It may involve conflict mediation from that middle position between the grass-roots and the top levels of society. It may involve attending to the institutions that need mending and rebuilding after a time of violence and war. It may involve lending what credibility we have as individuals and institutes to the strengthening of civil society. It may involve using the resources of our own networks to reconnect isolated societies with a larger world.

Third, it will involve articulating and then living a *spirituality of reconciliation* that is accessible to others and can be shared. The hard work of rebuilding broken societies will take more than plans to effect change. It takes a spirituality rooted in the memory of the crucified Christ and hopeful of the coming together of all things in the risen Lord to sustain us in the long and arduous work of reconciliation. For that reason, reconciliation is more of a spirituality than a strategy.

The spirituality of reconciliation has experienced the walk to Calvary with Christ. It has been conformed to the pattern of his death so that it might experience the power of the resurrection (Phil. 3:10). It is a spirituality that believes that forgiveness is possible, even though difficult. It is a forgiveness that does not forget the past, but has learned how to remember the past in a different way.

Conclusion

It seems to me that the Christian understanding of reconciliation could well provide both the resources and the very paradigm for a theology and spirituality of mission encountering a world marked by globalization. As with earlier paradigms of mission, it can be co-opted into a too easy accommodation with the world which it is trying to lead into God's reign. Just as mission in the time of colonialism could become a tool of the colonizers, or mission in the time of accompaniment could endorse ideologies inimical to the gospel, so too are there dangers with a paradigm of reconciliation. A concern for grace and mercy can fail to seek justice where it must come about, or confuse human achievement with God's action. But our lives in this world always involve this risk. We are constantly engaging a world that is both a creation of God and one tainted and twisted by the machinations of evil and the depredations of sin. Mission is not for the faint-hearted. It is for those whose hearts have been touched and healed by God's reconciling love, and who burn now that others might also experience it. In the often confusing, polycentric world that globalization has brought upon us, where the gaps between rich and poor yawn like unbridgeable abysses, it is important that we have that unshakable hope which St. Paul expressed in the eighth chapter of the Letter to the Romans:

> What will separate us from the love of Christ? Will anguish, or distress, or persecution, or famine, or nakedness, or peril, or the sword? . . . No, in all these things we conquer overwhelmingly through him who loved us. For I am convinced that neither death, nor life, nor angels, nor principalities, nor present things, nor future things, nor powers, nor height, nor depth, nor any other creature will be able to separate us from the love of God in Christ Jesus our Lord. (Rom. 8:35, 37-39)

That, I believe, is good news for the twenty-first century.

Response to Robert J. Schreiter, C.PP.S.

Peter Hünermann

ROBERT SCHREITER HAS MADE AN UTTERLY BASIC, FORWARD-looking contribution in his presentation. His well-documented and richly nuanced exposition of globalization as the context for today's missionary activity and his characterization of specific changes within the framework of globalization are of great significance for missionary efforts in the coming decades. His explanations also clearly show the limits and the limitations of the globalization process with which mission activity will have to contend. He makes an important plea to respond to the threats of globalization with corresponding means which globalization itself has at its disposal. His demonstration of how the structures of globalization can also be utilized on behalf of mission—the network of solidarity through communication, cooperation with the numerous NGOs, and the like—is also on the mark. Lastly, he has shown in his analysis of reconciliation how it should become the guiding theme for missionary activity in a world of conflict, with guilt on both sides.

This response to these rich and suggestive reflections will take up Schreiter's work and simply highlight and develop a few points implied in his exposition. This will be done in four steps.

1. We must recognize that the globalized world is one that is, to a great degree, divided and particularized. Or to put it more succinctly, the globalized world is a world of islands, extremely small islands. A few examples will serve to illustrate this thesis. Diplomats from the United States or a European country write many reports about the situation in the African or Latin American countries where they work. They may never have visited the large slums on the periphery of those cities. These areas are off-

limits to them. They cannot and must not ever go there. The life lived in those places is completely alien to them. They are familiar with the typical lifestyle of the rich who live in metropolitan São Paulo or Rio de Janeiro, cut off from the rest of the nation as effectively as if they lived on an isolated small island. These enclaves have their own drugstores, schools, physicians, and athletic centers. It is not even necessary to leave the enclave for the basic needs of life. These people live, as it were, sealed off from others, and they have absolutely no knowledge of the people and living conditions on the other side of the wall, and vice versa.

Such insular existence happens not only in such extreme instances. The Internet is opening up possibilities for global communication today. The professor in a European university can easily communicate with his counterpart in the United States. At the same time, however, the effect of these numerous possibilities for contact is that one must always make more choices. And these choices are increasingly determined by one's own interests and field of specialization. I would like to compare our situation in society with that found in industrial production. There, too, an ever-greater degree of differentiation has come into being. Think for a moment of the many specialized factories involved in the production and delivery of components destined to be installed in automobiles. One factory makes doors, another engine parts, and a third alternators. A high-level specialization is reflected in our societies as wholes, inasmuch as ever-expanding possibilities arising as a result of globalization create niches of special interest. The up-to-date information we receive daily through the news media cocoons us in the illusion that we are well-informed, that we know what is really going on. We are almost unaware that we are making choices. Perhaps we are even drowning in a flood of communication, but information is not the same as communication. In the original sense of the word, communication, *koinonia*, means that area enclosed by a wall or fence in which all the inhabitants of a village were allowed to graze their goats or cows. This "common ground," the prerequisite for any type of communication, is largely missing because the islands on which we are living in our globalized world do not have bridges to one another. Mission in the "global" world therefore means building such bridges. These bridges can come about only through the action of living human beings who cross over to the people of the other islands to create a living connection: missionaries, both men and women; groups such as Doctors without Borders, or Journalists without Borders.

2. The globalized world is an "instant world" in which the modern person painfully experiences slowness and the need for time for the things necessary for human life.

The globalized world is one characterized as much by instant coffee as by the possibility of instantaneous communication. Everything happens at breakneck speed. Expanses of space can be crossed in no time at all. Distances are drastically reduced. Yet at the same time the modern person in the globalized world notices how difficult and slow the process of rethinking things and changing one's long-established customs is. How hesitant and resistant are people to learn new ways of relating to one another.

I was with a group of students from Tübingen as guests at the only theological faculty in East Germany a few years after the Berlin Wall fell. The professors gave us some very interesting lectures about the history and present situation of the people in that formerly communist zone. They spoke of the great challenges of reunification. I recall quite well the statement of a philosopher who thought at the time that the over-forty generation would find it next to impossible to adapt to the new living conditions and to a competitive society with the demands it makes on the person. At the time I found this difficult to believe, and yet it has come true. Productivity in East German plants, despite the renovations in the industrial zones, is on the average 20 percent behind that in the West.

The experience of slowness, of toil, of the obdurate nature of so many things leads many people of our time to a feeling of powerlessness. Many people suffer from feelings of inadequacy; many are confused. This is true for the people of highly industrialized societies as well as for the people of Africa, Asia, and Latin America. In advance of the African Synod, a whole series of noteworthy studies discussed the often deep trauma, the feelings of inferiority, and the sense of hopelessness experienced by Africans. They are on the edge of despair because of the slow pace of the various stages of change in their conditions.

If the missionary proclamation of the good news is to help a person find the way to God, and thereby to his or her own self, then part of that proclamation must be accepting and acknowledging their slowness, their need for time. In our "instant" age, mission bears witness to the patience of God, to the slow growth of the kingdom of God among people.

3. The deepest and greatest threat to people in the globalized world is nihilism. The nihilism experienced by individuals in the globalized world is no longer the proud, grand nihilism (with a capital N) of which Nietzsche spoke, the nihilism of the person who sets himself up as absolute, fed by dreams of omnipotence. It is rather nihilism in a minor key, nihilism in the lower case. Today's lower-case nihilism is a result of the experience of insular existence, and of the difficulty and slowness of human change. It arises from the experience of helplessness in the face of networking global systems, and the seemingly unyielding pressure they produce. It befalls individuals as well as groups. An example of such hopelessness and loss of perspective leading to social explosiveness is what we find among Palestinians of our day. The great uprising of young people in Soweto in South Africa was an overwhelming sign of such loss of hope and perspective. Events taking place in Algeria arise from a similar situation of despair.

In their private lives, people seek comfort in the many little things in order to hide their own nihilism from themselves and from others. Only when people break out of their tightly bounded, exclusivist islands can God's horizons be opened up, can they experience that God is the "Master of the Impossible," as Charles de Foucauld put it.

This lower-case nihilism exists in church circles today as well. Many people live in isolation on tiny islands, never noticing that people beyond their circles are moved by the Spirit of God and live in faith. This type of experience is possible only for persons who reach out to others in their own situations. To me the introduction to the *motu proprio Ad tuendam fidem* seems to speak of such a despairing isolationism and nihilism, which it gives as one of the reasons why the church must be protected from theologians.

4. We discuss mission in the globalized and divided, particularized world.

Schreiter chose chapter 5 of the Second Letter to the Corinthians as an apt description of the missionary task today, where Paul speaks of reconciliation. In doing so he placed a very important emphasis on guidelines for today's missionary activity. I would like to look at the "how" of mission as described in Matthew 28. The text opens with the sentence "All power in heaven and on earth has been given to me." This is the basis of all missionary activity. It is accomplished in human infirmity, even in human impossibility. In Romans 14:9, Paul characterizes Jesus Christ's power as a lordship that derives from his self-giving on the cross. All missionary work is founded on this basis. In 2 Corinthians 5:14-15, it is stated quite clearly: reconciliation has been brought about by God in Christ. The next sentence begins "Go, therefore." In our day this means to go to the various worlds of our globalized society, cross over to the various islands that do not communicate with one another.

The next important statement is in Matthew 28:19: "make disciples . . . teaching." But what is to be taught. The message of the gospel is always credible when it is brought to people in ways of life that are marked by the gospel and in which it is obvious that here redeemed life is being imparted. Learning and teaching do not mean simply imparting the truths of the catechism. This is only the abstract, theoretical part. All these formulas become expressions of the gospel only if they are presented as a way of life, as lifestyles. It is not easy to create such faith-filled lifestyles, redeemed lifestyles, in our highly mobile, globalized society. The church's traditional forms developed to a great extent from the culture and lifestyle based on agriculture and manual labor. We are not suggesting anything new.

Finally, teaching in this way concludes with baptism in the name of the Father, and of the Son, and of the Holy Spirit. This baptism takes place at the time when individuals come into contact with witness to the faith, and through conversion to an authentic life and lifestyle imbued with the gospel, and suffused with the reality of God in their life.

Epilogue

Mission in the Third Millennium

Robert J. Schreiter, C.PP.S.

THE SEDOS CONGRESS PROVED TO BE AN EXCITING AND stimulating event. The discussion around the presentations made over a period of six days opened new vistas for mission as the church enters the third millennium. This concluding chapter tries to bring together some of the ideas that received special attention, both in the plenary sessions and in the discussion groups. It does not pretend to be an exhaustive account but rather highlights some of the salient and recurring themes that emerged during the Congress. As such, it gives some sense of the richness of conversation that took place, an overview of the issues that preoccupy people who are trying to think about the future mission, and insight into what may become the principal items on the missiological agenda in the next few decades.

These themes are grouped under five headings: the contexts of mission, the agents of mission, the shape of mission, missionary activity, and spirituality for mission. Let us look at each in turn.

The Contexts of Mission

Context has always been an important factor in the conduct of mission. It has not only helped or hindered the movements of missionaries, but has also had both favorable and unfavorable effects on the conduct of mission itself. Perhaps more than anything else, it was the linking of mission with European colonial adventures from the sixteenth to the twentieth centuries that heightened our sensitivity to the impact context can have on mission. In the 1960s and 1970s, in the immediate aftermath of the end of colonial empires, the question was raised whether mission itself could even be continued, given what appeared to be its inextricable embeddedness in the colonial adventure. But during that same time, under the impulse of the Second Vatican Council and in the fresh thinking coming out of Latin America, new possibilities began to emerge.

What are the salient elements of context interacting with mission today? A number of those elements received special attention during the Congress. First and foremost was the rise of globalization, especially during the 1990s. While contemporary globalization looks in many ways like the colonialism of the late nineteenth and early twentieth centuries—and its impact on the poor exhibits nearly the same characteristics as did colonialism—there are some significant differences, as I tried to point out in my presentation. What becomes imperative in this situation, then, as María Carmelita de Freitas said in her presentation, is to undertake a new analysis, lest we proffer old solutions to similar yet nonetheless significantly different problems. Globalization, for example, intensifies the sense of the local, whereas colonialism tended to minimize its significance. Colonialism had clear, identifiable agents; globalization's agents are often wrapped in anonymity. In all of this, it becomes important to develop responses that are commensurate with the causes.

The longer-term impact of globalization on the conduct of mission is still being assessed. It has been the cause of significant disruption in the lives of the poor. It also proffers a vision of the human that focuses on production and consumption as the measurements of genuine humanity. This is being sorted out in different ways, especially in Latin America and India.

A second significant shift in context is tied to what has become one of the effects of globalization, namely, the coincidence of religion and violence. Globalization has heightened the sense of the local, but also the sense of loss of control over the local, immediate environment in which people live. People then turn to religion to find some surer footing in the midst of the maelstrom that

globalization creates. Elements of difference are seized upon especially to foster clearer identities. The result is that religion
becomes invested with the means to create a more secure social
space. The boundaries around that social space are often not per-
meable. Other religious traditions are then extirpated from that
space. Christians have often been victims of this kind of interreligious violence, especially in parts of the world where they constitute a religious minority. Such violence is further fomented by
the fact that Christianity, given its colonial past, is identified with
the alienating forces of globalization arising in the West. But
Christians have themselves engaged in such violence, either
among themselves, or against other traditions, as examples from
Northern Ireland and the Balkans might show.

Michael Amaladoss explored this theme especially. The great
religious traditions have within them the resources both for promoting peacemaking and for abetting violence. Missionary situations where Christians are a small minority have become, in
many parts of the world, venues for violence. Efforts in teaching
and in ministry must focus on responding to violence and reducing the possibility of religion being used as a legitimation for violence. This is a theme that has taken on significant proportions at
the turn of the millennium, and more work will need to be done
on just how violence comes to nest in religion and feed upon religious passion. Equipping missionaries to deal with these situations of violence takes on new urgency.

A third shift in context, explored by Peter Hünermann, was the
advanced state of secularization of societies, especially as found
in Europe. Like de Freitas, he calls for a new analysis, especially
of church structures, to make the church more compatible and
credible to these kinds of societies. So much of the literature on
new evangelization in Europe is devoted to presenting (and often
decrying) the results of secularization. Little is focused on how
the church needs to change in order to meet the challenge. Hünermann is not advocating an utter accommodation of the church
to secular society; he notes also the incipient nihilism that weaves
its way through much of a secularized worldview. Yet is this not
simply a way of talking about the kind of inculturation which the
church in Europe (and other secularized parts of the world such
as Australia and North America) has to undertake? The paradox

is that, even as this secularization continues apace in certain regions of the world, one notes a resurgence of religion in other parts. Like the analysis called for in the case of the rise of globalization, theories of secularization are also being revisited. It is not the linear process of disenchantment which Max Weber suggested at the beginning of the twentieth century. The implications of how to address this for mission need greater attention.

A fourth instance of change in context was pointed to by Mercy Oduyoye: the growing strength of Islam in Africa. If Islam continues to grow as it has over the last thirty years, it will surpass Christianity as the world's largest religious tradition early in the twenty-first century. The encounters of Islam and Christianity have not always been peaceful. Parts of the Muslim world are struggling with the effects of modernization, especially concerning the antinomies between the values exhibited in modernization and those of Muslim faith. The failed promises about the benefits of modernization likewise become a source of contention. Christian–Muslim understanding becomes a major item on the agenda for mission in the new millennium.

In the discussion groups, a fifth theme surfaced also: the erosion of the physical environment, especially as it affects the poorest parts of the world. Care for the earth, a central religious theme since the Justice, Peace, and the Integrity of Creation project of the World Council of Churches in the 1970s, becomes a central aspect of mission in the twenty-first century.

How are these shifts in context changing mission? It may be yet too early to say for sure. The heightened conflicts in many parts of the world make reconciliation and peacemaking more important than may have been the case in the immediate past. Globalization has created greater poverty in many parts of the world, so concerns for justice become even greater. Heightened senses of the local can co-opt inculturation efforts for ideological purposes (i.e., inculturation becomes the way of legitimating ethnocentrism and nationalism). How modernization and secularization are unfolding in different societies around the world prompt a rethinking of mission in all of these settings. As was noted on several occasions, work has to be done in analyzing these new contexts and trying, as the new millennium unfolds, to draw from these analyses directions for mission.

The Agents of Mission

The presentations and the discussions focused on three sets of agents of mission: men and women religious, women more generally, and youth.

It is not surprising that a SEDOS meeting would attend especially to the role of religious in mission, since it is religious institutes that make up SEDOS. They have been the principal agents of mission, especially mission *ad gentes*, in the Roman Catholic Church. What is of importance as the new millennium begins is the changing demography of these religious institutes. The membership that will be active in the first half of the twenty-first century and beyond is coming from Africa, Asia, and to some extent from Latin America, rather than the North Atlantic region and Australia. The financial resources, however, are still lodged largely in the latter regions. The changing demography is already being expressed in the makeup of general governments. But how will this change the institutes themselves, and how mission will be carried out?

What is becoming evident is that two perspectives are evolving within religious institutes about their future character. Members especially from Europe are concerned about how the charism of their institute is being transmitted: Do members in Asia, Africa, and Latin America really understand the charism? Members in those areas, however, raise a different concern: the need for better intercultural communication. Behind each of these concerns is a larger issue about how identities are being forged. Members from "older" regions worry about whether the importance of the origins of the institute is being faithfully transmitted. Members from the "younger" regions feel that much of what goes under the rubric of charism is really European culture, and that their cultures are not being accorded the same respect. This is a major challenge facing all international religious institutes, but especially international missionary religious institutes.

Going with these issues of identity is also the conduct of mission. Will the large financial resources many missionary religious institutes enjoy reach far into the twenty-first century? How will missionaries conduct themselves and their mission? Does the socialization of poor candidates into a largely middle-class stratum best prepare them for work among the poor? Do people coming out of colonized settings conduct mission differently from those who come from colonizing countries? These are questions that the demographic shifts in international missionary institutes raise in an acute fashion; we are seeking to answer them by sustaining the dialogue between the different regions of the world.

Mercy Oduyoye pointed especially to the importance of women in general in mission. This becomes a question not only because of their sheer number, but also because they are being emancipated from the restrictions which patriarchal societies have placed on their roles. Will distinctly women's ways of doing mission emerge more clearly in the coming years, moving beyond their traditional roles in education and healthcare? Will, for example, women take greater leadership roles in devising ways of reconciliation and social reconstruction in post-conflict areas of the world? Again, this is an area to be attended to in the years ahead.

On a number of occasions, the group discussions raised questions about youth. Each generation is formed by different social and ecclesial events. It was clear throughout the presentations and the discussions that the Second Vatican Council and its aftermath and the activism of the 1960s had been formative events for many of the participants at the Congress. Sr. de Freitas's presentation focused on that formation explicitly for religious. What of the generation now coming of age and entering missionary work, who were born after those events? What shapes their horizon? How do they perceive the world in its variety and its challenges? Because SEDOS is constituted by the general governments of missionary institutes—men and women typically between forty-five and sixty years of age—the voices of youth were not present. But this did not prevent their potential impact from being felt. Yet youth, of course, hold the future—and the future of mission—in their hands. It has already been noted that young missionaries are coming overwhelmingly from the Southern Hemisphere. Again, this is an area that will require careful observation and dialogue in the immediate years ahead.

One group of agents was not discussed as directly, namely, lay missionaries who accept a fixed term of commitment (although many renew their terms multiple times). These missionaries are coming especially from the First World areas. There appears to be no sign of the diminishment of their numbers, as is the case among members of religious institutes. Their continued presence in mission has to be factored into any scenario for mission in the new millennium.

Looking at the agents of mission is always an important part of considering the future of mission. After all, it is *people* who engage in mission. Moreover, the agents of mission give us a window into the immediate future of mission, since the people who will be engaging in mission are now already beginning or are in formation. Those just beginning mission will be in positions of leadership in missionary institutes in the next decade. The formative experiences they are having will shape the direction of mission in the future.

The Shape of Mission

Do changes in the context and the personnel of mission augur any changes in the overall shape of mission? Mission for Roman Catholics after the Second Vatican Council and after the end of colonial empires took on a strong sense of the *accompaniment* of people through dialogue, inculturation, and the liberation of the poor—something amply documented at the 1981 SEDOS Seminar. While this sense of accompaniment did not supersede earlier notions of mission as proclamation and development through education and healthcare, there was a resoundingly different tone set in the second half of the twentieth century. Does the opening of the twenty-first century hold out a new direction?

A new direction might be on the horizon. A number of the speakers referred to the *missio Dei*—the mission of God—a term that came into currency in the 1930s. Karl Barth was one of the first to use the term, and it came into widespread use in the 1950s. *Missio Dei* may be coming back with a somewhat modified meaning. In view of the many difficult, seemingly intractable, issues mission is facing—conflict, interreligious violence, growing poverty and hunger, loss of local control, erosion of the physical environment—there seems to be a growing awareness that it is not that we carry out mission, but rather that we participate in what is first and foremost God's work. This is, of course, an idea worked out in the doctrinal foundations in *Ad Gentes*, in which the trinitarian character of mission is emphasized. But after a period of confident activism in mission, mission's other pole (i.e., its connection to God) is coming more clearly into view today. This does not mean a passivity before matters of social justice or a quietism that eschews social engagement. It is rather a different attitude toward the relationships within mission. The renewed focus on God's activity can become a source of hope for beleaguered missionaries who see so much of their work coming to naught. It may, therefore, have special relevance today as we face postconflict situations that cry out for reconciliation and social reconstruction, where the poor have less control over their lives than ever, and where disruption in social life looms especially large. In all of these situations, what needs to be done seems to be beyond our ability to bring about. It is in such situations that we come to recognize how much the transforming work of mission is first and foremost God's work.

The strong interest in missionary spirituality seems to reflect this emphasis on the *missio Dei*. The missionary's relationship with God is taking a central place in discussion of mission in ways it has not in the recent past (more will be said about this below). An emphasis on our participation in the work of God does not deny or represent a retreat from the intense activism of the recent past, but it may be offering a way of recovering more clearly the vertical dimension in mission. It may be a kind of corrective to fill out more completely the shape of mission as our accompaniment, especially of the poor, in bringing the good news.

Missionary Activity

The 1981 SEDOS Research Seminar proposed that missionary activity takes place under four headings: proclamation, dialogue, inculturation, and liberation of the poor. All four of these activities continue to be valid. Looking at them at the turn of the twenty-first century, we see them as being nuanced or directed slightly differently, mainly because the contexts in which they are done continue to change.

Acts of proclamation (as reaffirmed in the encyclical *Redemp-*

toris Missio in 1990) continue to be at the center of missionary activity. Imparting the good news, giving an account of the things we hope for, is a vital component of missionary activity. What may be clearer in our current situation is the variety of forms which proclamation needs to take. The preaching in the Acts of the Apostles has usually been taken as the prototype. The presentations and the discussions at the Congress suggested some forms of proclamation perhaps more specific to the early twenty-first century.

Two forms of proclamation are suggested by the context of globalization. The first is the denunciation of the idolatrous use of religious concepts by economic globalization to legitimate its activities in quasi-religious fashion. This is found most frequently today in the literature coming from Latin America; Sr. de Freitas refers to it extensively in her presentation. Idolatry may be a bigger problem than atheism in the contemporary world, suggesting that human beings seek out forms of deity even when they appear to be denying it. This is an important form of proclamation—to denounce the false gods being presented as absolutes and the inevitable.

The second form of proclamation is found in solidarity and resistance. In his discourses on globalization, Pope John Paul II repeatedly refers to the necessity of solidarity with the poor in the face of economic globalization. Solidarity among those likely to be excluded, and a solidarity that counteracts the nihilism of secularized societies (one might add also the nihilism in some post-Communist societies as well) is a reaffirmation of the dignity of each human person. Similarly, there are aspects of globalization that call for resistance as well inasmuch as they diminish human beings and militate against human existence as meaningful and purposive. Such resistance is another form of denunciation of forces that dehumanize social life. Resistance can also take more positive forms, such as the opening up of social spaces where reconciliation can take place, where people might gather to imagine alternatives to the current situation, where hope can be born and nurtured.

Dialogue is also in a different place than it was a few decades ago. Both of the presentations from the Asian context, but especially Sung-Hae Kim's, underscored dialogue as the way of evangelization in Asia. The threefold dialogue urged by the Federation of Asian Bishops' Conferences—dialogue with religions, dialogue with cultures, dialogue with the poor—maps out what needs to be done on that great continent. Dialogue is a form of witness and opens the path to understanding. In recent years, it has become increasingly clear that dialogue is the only way to greater world peace, especially in those regions where religious difference is used to inflame populations and foster violence. In these settings, dialogue is essential for human survival and human thriving.

Dialogue continues to be misunderstood in some sectors as an alternative to proclamation or to mission itself. But the message to be emphasized over and over again is that dialogue is, in some places like Asia, simply the way the good news of Jesus Christ can likely be heard and understood. It connotes respect for the other party and for the truth all sides are seeking. It is the more respectful and effective way to communicate in many cultures. For dialogue to be done well, the spirituality of those dialoguing must be transparent.

Another feature for the dialogue of religions is the need for Christians to become more acquainted with the traditions with which they hope to dialogue. Sung-Hae Kim illustrated that well in her presentation. Ignorance of the traditions in the setting in which Christians find themselves is something that can no longer be excused.

Inculturation as a form of mission has perhaps been more honored as a concept than as a practice. To that extent, inculturation remains an idea yet to be tried in many places. Sung-Hae Kim's suggestions for the inculturation of missionary religious institutes in Confucian settings show what kind of work needs to be done. An equally serious challenge facing inculturation today is its misuse as a way to legitimate ethnocentrism or nationalism, creating a form of local Christianity that is intolerant and sometimes even hostile to others. As has already been noted, Hünermann's analysis of the situation of the church in contemporary Europe is indeed a call for a new inculturation of Christianity in that part of the world. He suggests reforms in church structures that will allow the gospel to take root more easily in that part of the world. Without even having the possibility to take root, it can never raise that critical, prophetic voice that can lead to a genuine evangelization of cultures.

Working for the liberation of the poor is a continuing priority of mission. As was already noted in the first section, the analysis that informed these efforts in the 1970s and 1980s needs to be revisited. The shape of this new analysis is not entirely clear, especially as to what should be the modes of response. Globalization as the driving force is much more elusive than the national security state as the place for encounter and interaction. Yet we cannot give up on finding new ways to engage the gospel message effectively with globalization and its effects.

All in all, then, one can see how missionary activity shifts because of changed circumstances. Different emphases emerge. Older approaches may or may not continue, but usually with a different perspective. Keeping track of those shifts is an important part in giving leadership to missionary institutes, since such adjustments are continually necessary if the gospel is truly to be heard and engaged.

Missionary Spirituality

As missionaries move into the new millennium, it is clear that the issue of spirituality has a high priority. As was suggested above, this may have to do with another perspective on mission that is emerging, namely, mission as first and foremost the work of God. Elements of missionary spirituality appear in the presentations offered here (such as in Kim's discussion of what it means to seek the will of God together, and in Sr. de Freitas's use of the story of Jesus and the Samaritan woman at the well from John 4), but it was especially in the discussion groups that interest in spirituality could be found.

Two ideas frequently mentioned were a spirituality of presence, and a kenotic spirituality. Sung-Hae Kim spoke of presence as more than simply being in a situation; it connotes an active, but not intrusive engagement—being present-to and present-for. It is an attitude that is nurtured especially by contemplative prayer and by meditation. The rediscovery of the contemplative dimension of missionary spirituality appears to be one of the emerging elements in mission in the third millennium. Why that is the case at this time may have something to do with the overwhelming challenges facing missionaries because of conflict, the need for reconciliation, and the sense of helplessness in the face of the forces of globalization. It may arise too with the experience of burnout, or of the loss of religious focus in struggles for liberation. Certainly any missionary activity having a focus on dialogue will be attentive to the interior dimension that must inform and direct genuine dialogue.

Closely connected to presence was a recurrent turning to *kenosis,* or self-emptying. Modeled on the great christological hymn in Philippians 2:5-11, where the Logos sets aside divinity and takes on becoming human, in the form of a slave. *Kenosis* speaks of the opposite of human power. It seeks rather the power of God, manifested in the suffering Christ on the cross. Again, one sees how this might be connected to the *missio Dei,* where the mission of the Second Person of the Trinity is precisely that of *kenosis.* This concept of missionary spirituality is meaningful, too, in view of the fact that missionaries heretofore have largely come from rich and powerful countries, and must empty themselves if they are truly to be among (rather than over) the people whom they encounter. As the demography of missionaries changes, will thoughts about kenosis change as well? It seems likely not, since the larger forces spoken of above (conflict, globalization, and the like) continue to shape the context in which missionaries work. Kenosis (and presence) will continue to be appropriate forms of spirituality to working in such contexts.

Because of the great amount of interest in reconciliation at this point in history, a spirituality of reconciliation, informed especially by scriptural passages such as 2 Corinthians 5:17-20 and Ephesians 2:12-22, is finding its way into missionary spirituality. This spirituality shares characteristics of the kenotic spirituality just noted: it sees reconciliation first and foremost as the work of God; we are but the agents through whom God works. It sees God beginning the work of reconciliation with the healing of the victim, rather than focusing on the wrongdoer.

A fourth theme that is just beginning to appear is a greater focus on anthropology, the Christian vision of the human. This was prompted by trying to engage Confucianism more directly in East Asia and by countering the dehumanizing aspects of globalization. Sr. de Freitas's call for a more holistic anthropology and Kim's delineation of what Christianity offers to a Confucian worldview (the importance of grace, the dignity of the individual person, and the meaning of the cross in the face of naive optimism) point us in fruitful directions for continuing to explore this important element.

The discussion groups repeatedly raised the question of the ongoing formation of current missionaries and the formation of the next generation of missionaries. Again, such is to be expected from members of the general government of missionary institutes, who are charged with maintaining and transmitting the charism of their respective institutes. It no doubt arises also out of care for those members of their institutes who experience difficulty in their missionary work, either because of the situations in which they find themselves (such as situations of violence) or because of burnout. All in all, however, a general awareness that missionary spirituality is something that needs much closer attention than it has been given in the past thirty or so years has clearly emerged on the horizon.

Conclusion

So where does all of this lead as Christian mission enters a new millennium? With significant changes in the context and in the agents of mission, some rethinking of the shape of mission, of forms of missionary activity, and what is needed to sustain people in mission is inevitable. One certainly detects themes continuing from earlier periods. Other themes are offering new challenges. One can also note certain earlier themes, such as the trinitarian foundations of mission, as coming now to new fruition in thinking on the *missio Dei*. Finally, new analyses, prompted by globalization and by the current form of secularization will be needed. All in all, as mission enters a new millennium, one can detect new areas for research and action, prompted not so much by the turn of the calendar as by the larger events in history and in the shifting populations that greet us as we enter the twenty-first century.

Index